MANIFESTING
ME

—

MANIFESTING ME

ME

—

A STORY OF REBELLION AND REDEMPTION

—

LEAH E. REINHART

SHE WRITES PRESS

Published 2018
Printed in the United States of America
ISBN: 978-1631523830 paperback
978-1-63152-384-7 ebook

Library of Congress Control Number: 2017963221

Book design by Stacey Aaronson

For information, address:
She Writes Press
1563 Solano Ave #546
Berkeley, CA 94707

She Writes Press is a division of SparkPoint Studio, LLC.

I dedicate this book to my daughter, Samantha.
You saved me from a path of self-destruction and inspired me to
want a better life and to be a better person through love.

PREFACE

My son asked me, "Why would anyone read this story? You aren't famous." He's right; I'm not famous, but everyone has a unique story, and I'm here to share mine. I believe, as many others do, that we are all on this planet to learn and to share our gifts. We are here to explore and become the highest selves we can be. Everyone plays a part, whether they came to this planet to be the hero, the victim, or the villain. After all, someone has to be the bad guy, and it's usually the most upsetting experiences that teach us and help us to evolve the most, reaching inward instead of thinking that the outside world will make us whole. This is a story about overcoming normal and not-so-normal obstacles in life.

The outside world is only a perception. I cannot express that strongly enough. Being dyslexic, my perception is very different. My eyes do not always see what's in front of me. I might spell a familiar word and leave out the last letter, even though my brain thinks it is there. Not to mention how our brains fill in gaps. For example, our peripheral vision is mostly colorblind, with few color receptors. When it comes to our sense of taste, why is one thing spicy hot to one person and mild to another? It's all perception.

So, who is telling the truth? Each individual has his or her own truth. My point is that this is just my story and my perception of it. After all, if you spoke to my sister . . . well, let's just say we grew up completely differently. I don't blame anyone; in fact, I thank everyone for playing their parts to help me fulfill my destiny, the reason I came to Earth school. While writing this, I've come to realize there are themes in all these little stories of life's challenges and triumphs. Some of these themes include overcoming fear, dealing with rejection, learning patience, and feeling accepted, which are very common for most people.

I believed that my achievements would bring me happiness. Although they did for a while, all things outside of us are only temporary. We feel joy when something is going well in our lives, and we feel sorrow or pain when we experience something negative. I guess that's a no-brainer. All these things are temporary and are usually outside of us. For example, chocolate tastes wonderful to most of us and releases endorphins, but the feeling goes away once the chocolate is gone. You might feel nice and relaxed after a glass of wine, but it too wears off. Being in love is one of the most wonderful feelings, but what happens when it's not reciprocated? What I am trying to say in this story is that peace, joy, and love come from within. You don't need another person to complete you or make you feel loved. You don't need alcohol or drugs to relax you. You can and are entitled to feel this love and peace all on your own. As in *The Wizard of Oz*, you don't need a diploma to tell you that you have a brain, you don't need a testimonial to know that you can feel love and have compassion, and you don't need a medal to show that you can have courage. There are basically two emotions: fear and love. Sometimes, our teachers (meaning people who are put in our lives, like family members, friends, or mentors, not just in the classroom) don't always know how to teach without instilling fear. Love is always the way.

Also, this story is about not comparing your story with someone else's. I watch Oprah's *Super Soul Sunday* (which I love), and she has the most inspiring people who tell amazing stories. Things like losing your limbs and still being an Olympian, or going on a journey through the mountains alone. All are wonderful stories. Those people truly have a gift to share with the world. Their experiences are meant to help people and motivate them to overcome obstacles in their lives.

But what about the average person? We all still have to come to the same conclusion as they did. The extraordinary person shows that anyone can do it. I have found that a lot of people minimize their problems because they observe others suffering even more. Problems are problems, no matter how big or how small, to the person experiencing them. For example, I have a friend with a very lucrative business who, nevertheless, worries about not having enough money, the same way a person earning minimum wage worries about losing his or her home; it's the same theme. I've learned through many years of therapy not to make light of my issues; in fact, that's really a way of ignoring your issues. When you are in denial about your feelings and they need to be released, they will come out in all sorts of negative, self-destructive ways.

So here's a story, not too extraordinary, about overcoming the same problems as the extraordinary person. It's been said, though I can't remember by whom, "The three toxic Cs are complaining, competing, and comparing."

All the names have been changed to protect the innocent and the not so innocent.

Sometimes I'm not sure what "normal" means to the rest of the world. We all wonder what makes us the people we are and why we respond in certain ways to certain situations. Well, I believe there are many circumstances involved in creating our motives and responses. After all, that is one of life's many great mysteries. Why do we sometimes have to go through shit? Why can't every day be filled with candy and roses? It took me a while to appreciate the crazy drama I grew up in, but I can definitely say I have lived and experienced an eventful life.

Life lessons aren't something that you just learn and say, "Next!" It's an ongoing thing, a sort of evolution, if you will, like the song, "Looking for Love in All the Wrong Places." Everyone has a unique and interesting story to tell. I just felt compelled to write the story about my many challenges, for some strange reason. Maybe it was this path of crazy situations that led me to write this book of my experiences. Nevertheless, I'm here to share and hopefully touch some lives or, at the very least, to entertain you.

Chapter 1

THE EAST BAY

I was born in Hayward, California, in 1969, and my family lived there until I was six years old. I have one sister, Nicole. She is three years older and has a very different personality from mine. We lived in a house on a great street where there were many kids and where it was safe to walk alone just about anywhere. Our neighbors were mostly a lot of fun, and we did your typical kids' stuff. My favorite activity was swimming. We belonged to a swim club just around the corner from our house, and I started lessons when I was three years old. Many happy times were had in the neighborhood pool.

I was born into a very stoic family, whereas I am an extremely emotional person and somewhat of an empath, which made me feel that I didn't fit in with my family. I was also one of those clingy children who would hang on to my mother's leg. I was always acutely aware of my surroundings; I observed everything around me and took it all in. I was known for being the crybaby of the family and a little bit of a "scaredy cat." I was frightened of so many things: dogs, boys, the street cleaner, loud helicopters. I would hear lots of noises, especially at night, and sometimes see weird images on the hallway wall, which led to my sleeping with the covers pulled over my head. My sister was quite the opposite. She wasn't afraid of anything that I could recall. My mom described her as the one to stand up to anyone, regardless of their size, if there was something that didn't sit right with her. She was definitely not afraid of any sort of confrontation, the way I was.

I had a lot of bossy friends. Kids got me to do all sorts of things. My sister and her friend, who lived across the street and was a bit of a shit stirrer, got me to try to smoke a cigarette when I was just four years old. Then, in kindergarten, when I was deathly afraid of boys, my so called "friend" Deanna wanted me to kiss a boy in class. She told me that she wouldn't be my friend anymore if I didn't do it. So, of course, I had to kiss him under the table in class. I felt humiliated. I didn't like being controlled, but I so desperately wanted to be accepted.

Anyway, I'm sure you know how the story goes. Kids need to figure out how they fit into this crazy world. So the peer pressure begins. You have the leaders, the followers, and the loners. I wasn't sure where I fit in yet, but it was looking like I might be a follower. Peer pressure influenced me everywhere and for a very long time.

I'm not sure where, why, or when I began to feel so unsafe or when I developed such a strong desire to fit in and please everyone, but it might have had something to do with our crazy neighbors, the Ellings family, who had moved in next door and who were just plain weird. The man was not nice, and the woman was pregnant at the time. The man took his anger and frustration out on his wife and dog. I heard yelling coming from their house, but, being so young at the time, I was unfamiliar with domestic violence.

The Ellings also taunted my mother. They would take pictures of our house for unknown reasons, and they cranked up their music so loud that our house would boom from the bass. To this day, I hate hearing that kind of music. It takes me back to those uneasy and anxious feelings.

Finally, my mom called the cops, and they told her to file a complaint, but it did nothing. Then, one day, Mrs. Ellings turned up at our house. When she came to the door, my mom opened it, but left the chain on so it couldn't open all the way. She was accusing my mom of something, I'm not sure of what, but I was getting pretty scared. I can remember it as if it were yesterday. She was actually pushing the door in to try to break the chain. Then my mother realized that the garage door was open, so she ran to the garage to close it. While my mom was trying to shut the door, that evil woman actually hit her. My mom wasn't a fighter to begin with, but Mrs. Ellings was also pregnant, so my mom wouldn't have considered hitting her back. Mom just screamed and cried, and I noticed that she was shaking, which terrified me.

Maybe that was the beginning of my not feeling safe or protected by anyone. No one ever checked on me to see if I was okay—which I clearly wasn't. Regardless, it was a traumatic experience for a five-year-old, and the point at which I really began to hate mean people. That incident was also the deciding factor in our leaving Hayward and moving to Oakland.

MOVING TO OAKLAND

Getting back to their roots seemed to be the perfect fit for my parents. Both of them had grown up in Oakland and enjoyed their youth, but by the time they wanted to move back it was the seventies and things were pretty different. Oakland has long had a reputation for being one the most violent cities in the United States. Oakland in the sixties and seventies was known for a lot of racially motivated riots, and the crime rate was off the charts. It also had some of the lowest scoring public schools in the country.

Despite all that, our neighborhood, Holy Hill—so-called because of the many churches between 98th Avenue and Joaquin Miller—looked awesome. It was like moving to the country. I felt a sense of peace, for once. There were so many great trees for tree houses, trails for hiking, barns, horses, corrals, huge backyards, and you weren't right on top of your neighbors. It was heaven-sent. There was, and still is, a lot of wildlife, which would end up being one of my many passions.

We moved in, I believe, two days before Christmas in 1975. Mom made sure to have the Christmas tree up, so that the holiday would go on as usual. She decorated our artificial tree the same way year after year, the glass ball ornaments strategically placed so as not to have too many of the same color next to each other. She draped the gold tinsel garland around the tree perfectly. We had beautiful colored flower lights that made the tree absolutely brilliant. Mom was awesome at making each holiday special. Holidays were the best in my house. Needless to say, this Christmas was just like any other Christmas, but it was in a new, much better location, although there were only a few houses that had Christmas trees or Christmas lights, and that seemed odd.

———

I'll never forget meeting the other kids who lived on Holy Hill. Back in the day when we didn't have all the tech devices we have today, kids always knew how to seek each other out in any situation. Right after we moved in, I saw a girl with long, blonde hair standing across from our driveway. She must have seen the moving truck go by her house. The girl was wearing a denim skirt, a T-shirt, and old tennis shoes, and she was standing with her big, furry, male collie. I was terrified of dogs, but Nicole and I went over to the girl and introduced ourselves.

The girl's name was Rosie Hall. She lived down the street from us and was ten years old, just a few months older than Nicole. She had one brother and three sisters. We weren't used to big families like that. Rosie took Nicole and me to her house to meet her family. Their house was very small for a family of seven. I noticed the girls all wore skirts and had very long hair, like something straight out of *Little House on the Prairie*. I couldn't tell if they were wearing Gunne Sax dresses or if they were handmade. It was almost like going into a time warp, and I wasn't sure if that was good or bad. I thought they were weird, but there was also a niceness about them. They seemed like a warm and inviting family. And all I knew was that I couldn't stand mean people.

I also might have been a little jealous. I thought it would have been great to have a big family—not to mention some protection from all the things that scared me. My sister really didn't want me around much. If I'd had a big brother who could have kept me safe or a younger sister who'd wanted to play with me, that would have been a dream come true.

Of the Hall kids, Lexi was the closest to my age—one year younger than I. Ellen was about three years younger, Claire was the baby, and Sawyer was the only boy and much older, in his early teens. Apparently, it paid to be a boy in his family, because we soon discovered he was treated like a king. As intuitive as I was, I got the definite impression that men were considered superior in that family. Sawyer liked to torment Lexi. He had a dirt bike and used to chase her with it, as if he were going to run her over. I remember wondering, *Why is he so mean to her? He doesn't treat his other siblings that way.* One day, I went to see if she could play, and she was up a wall near her garage, crying hysterically, and there he was, revving his motorcycle and laughing. I didn't like or trust him, but since I was friends with Lexi and knew I might be targeted, I never said anything to him.

There were a few other boys in the neighborhood. Most of them were much older, and it seemed as if all the boys had motorcycles or dirt bikes. It was very important not to get in their way when they rode up and down the street, and they were loud and obnoxious. For a girl of only six, it was a lot to take in.

MAN'S BEST FRIEND, TAKEN TO A WHOLE NEW LEVEL

There were more dogs than people in the neighborhood, and they were all different breeds, from small, ratty dogs to Irish wolfhounds to the Saint Bernard and the collie that Rosie's family had. No dog had ever bitten me, but I used to scream anytime a dog got near me. One day, I set off walking down the hill to go exploring, and, when I got to the third house on the right, this big black dog came running out, barking ferociously and charging me. Of course, I ran . . . home that is. I told Mom and she said, "Never let the dog know you're scared. Yell 'Knock it off!' and be confident." I guess she knew about dog behaviorist Cesar Milan's theory a long time ago. So off I went, back down the hill, and tried it out. Of course, the dog came charging out again, but I stood my ground. I couldn't believe my mom was right. That was such an empowering moment.

I had this sensation of power and confidence. That dog backed down. Never let 'em see you sweat, right? I have to admit that I was a little afraid that it wouldn't work, but I yelled in a firm, though shaky, voice, "Go home! Get!" and it worked! I thought, *How cool! I got this.* Little did I know that would be a major life lesson, facing my fears. Thank goodness, my need to have friends and to get out of the house would aid in my overcoming some of my fears. Being a determined person might have something to do with it, as well.

Fundamentally, though, I was a timid and easily frightened little girl. Among all these scary dogs and crazy, loud boys, I knew somehow that I was going to have to change, even though change was also a very scary prospect to me— and I hadn't even started school yet.

Chapter 2

HOOD RATS

When winter break was over, my mom registered Nicole and me in our new school. I was a little nervous about it, but what can you do when you're only six years old? I remember going to the office and thinking, *Wow, there are a lot of African American people.* I'd never seen so many in my life. After all, Hayward was all Caucasian and Hispanic. So my mom just about died when I said to this African American woman registering her child, "Wow! There are sure a lot of black people here." The lady was super nice and just laughed a little. I ended up being friends with her daughter.

The first day of school was very different. The children were not like the ones I was used to. They said a lot of bad words, and you were warned never to go to the bathroom. Apparently, that was not a safe place. There were rumors of girls and boys getting jumped in there. I'm not even sure where these rumors came from, but you didn't want to tempt fate. I got a lot of my information from listening to and observing what people were saying and doing around me. Plus, I heard people talking about fights that happened in the bathrooms. Since the teachers or yard duty people paid little attention to the kids on the playground while they were supposed to be watching us, I didn't trust them at all, especially since they never went into the bathrooms. I knew I didn't want to meet up with any bigger kids in the bathroom without any witnesses, so I learned to hold it all day. That could be why I have some stomach issues to this day.

The second day of school, a new white girl named Isabella started. She had come from another school that was even tougher than our school, and she had an attitude. She and I were the newbies at school, so we clicked and eventually became best friends. She was the bossy type, a typical Capricorn, but I didn't mind being bossed all that much as I am a passive Pisces. After all, my mom was a Capricorn, too.

Isabella lived with her mom, Vicki, and her mom's boyfriend, Darnell. Her biological dad had died in the Vietnam War, so she had never met him. Darnell was a good-looking, light-skinned black man with beautiful green eyes, but there was a definite air about him, and I don't mean a good one. He just seemed mean and violent, as if he could snap and hit you at any moment—kind of like Sawyer. Behind those pretty eyes was an untrustworthiness. I, naturally, was a little leery around him.

Vicki was quite the opposite. She was sweet, kind, and loving, more a hippie type. She was an RN, which suited her perfectly. Her vibe and aura was one that I wanted to be around. She was so easygoing. I really loved her and felt an immediate connection with her. Vicki had a way of making me feel safe when I was around her, which definitely was not the case at school.

It seemed as if we had the tough kids from all walks of

life at our school. Kids are mean, and they will look for any kind of weakness to use to their advantage. I remember when one of my classmates, Fat Matt, took one of those red rubber balls and just beamed it off my head, almost knocking me out. I think Fat Matt was an Angel brat. Rumor had it that a lot of the white kids were Hells Angels' kids, and there weren't all that many white kids to begin with.

To make matters worse, I was in no way a fighter, even though I had grown up with one: my sister, Nicole. She wasn't afraid of anyone, and she could be mean, if you were brave enough to challenge her. I should have known that I'd be tough just by living with her. She liked fighting for fun. It was more like sparring, and she didn't think she'd ever really get hurt. The joy of growing up around that.

My friend Isabella was equally powerful and good at ma-nipulating people. All she had to say was, "I'm not going to be your friend," or, "What's the matter with you? You a chicken?" That would get me every time. I couldn't be known as a chicken. And I couldn't lose any friends; I needed all the friends I could get. After all, talking and playing with kids my age was my whole social life. You could pretty much talk me into anything and everything, as long as it didn't kill me. I did have some sense of self-preservation. For example, I hate heights, so climbing trees posed a challenge, but, still, I'd be up that tree, trembling and all. Sometimes I would just have to jump out of the tree and hope for the best. Climbing up was much easier than coming back down. Nothing like peer pressure to help conquer your fears.

I was also determined to learn how to ride a bike. At the house in Hayward, Nicole had an orange Schwinn bike with big ape hanger handlebars, but, no matter how hard I tried to ride that stupid bike, it was just too big and dangerous for me. It always managed to somehow inflict pain on me, whether I was by myself or riding with someone else, which made it even worse. One of the best things about our new house was that it came with a green Schwinn Stingray bike that was just my size. I practiced every day and mastered it pretty quickly. I was up and riding, finally, without injury. It was a proud moment. It felt so good to accomplish a hard task.

I'll never forget when Larissa, one of the toughest girls in school, told me to never be a "mark." That meant if you didn't stand up for yourself, no matter if you won or lost, you would be targeted forever. I knew the day would come when I too would have to face that horrible challenge. But what would be worse, fighting once or always being picked on? That's pretty messed up when you're only seven years old.

As I said before, my school was different. When the boys chased you, it wasn't like what normal kids do. The boys at this school would dry hump you if they caught you. That probably was where my track career started. I didn't want to be caught. I also remember these two boys in a precarious position behind the portable cafeteria. Definitely didn't look right and everyone made fun of them. Said things like "Eww, they're freakin' each other." I learned real quickly what sex was. The kids at school talked about it all the time, and I just couldn't believe that what they were saying was true. They said my parents had to have to sex in order for me to be here. *That's disgusting. My parents wouldn't have done that. That's gross.* Naturally, I had to ask my mother about this nonsense. She went into a whole technical explanation that I eventually tuned out. But I finally got confirmation that, in fact, it was true.

———

Being on the hill was very different from school life. Most of the people that lived on the hill belonged to the same ultra-conservative church, and they all seemed like they were country people, which was very different than how the kids from school lived. On the hill there were horses, chickens, and so many animals. And let's not forget all the dogs. There was so much wildlife around: snakes, lizards, scorpions, bobcats, foxes, and goats that had gone feral. You name it, and it was there. It was like a mini-vacation every day. I would go hiking up in the hills and just felt free and safe. None of us really thought about mountain lions or coyotes. I think they were farther out in the wild space back then.

Sometimes some of the neighbors would let their horses roam free on the hill to graze. Somehow, we met this young woman, Lindsay, who gave horseback riding lessons, and soon my sister and I were riding. Lindsay was nearly twenty, and she was a wild one, at least by church standards. I really liked her. We went twice a week. She had us put the saddle on, brush the horse, and do everything we needed to do to get the horse ready for riding. We learned everything we could about how to take care of the animal. I can't believe at seven years old I was picking up the saddle and putting it on by myself.

Of course, being my timid self, I was also afraid of horses. Actually, I was more afraid of falling off. After all, horses are really big animals, and I was pretty small at seven years old. Sometimes, Lindsay's horse, Dandy, would take off on us. This horse was one of the smartest horses you'd ever meet. She would do anything for food, including trying to work a combination lock with her teeth. Eventually, I learned how to ride a horse, and I didn't die when I fell off. It only felt like it when the wind got knocked out of me. And believe me, I have fallen many times, but, fortunately, I never really got hurt. Back then we didn't even have helmets. All those lessons led to many trail rides and adventures. We roamed through the Oakland hills all the way to Castro Valley and Moraga. It was very freeing for such a young kid.

Later, Isabella found out I was taking horseback riding lessons, and she wanted to take them too. So she'd come to my house, and we would go to her lesson together. We always cut across the hillside, which was easier than going on the street with its many steep hills. It was much like the song, "Over the River and Through the Woods."

I had a love-hate relationship with the woods. They were so cool in the daytime, but not so much at night. They were pretty dark during the day, so you can imagine how dark they were after the sun went down. It was either take the long way home or suck it up and challenge yourself to see what you're made of. Of course, I ran as fast as I could go, because who knew what could possibly be in there? One time I got a face full of spiderwebs. Back in those days our parents would let us stay out until dark, or maybe until eight, as long as we got our homework finished. Once the clocks were set back, it was dark early, and we didn't have a lot of streetlights on our hill. We would sometimes try to catch a ride with my dad when he came home from work, because the hills were so steep and we were feeling a little bit lazy. But I'd rather be playing or hanging out with my friends than get a ride from my dad. After all, there was another hour or two left.

FIRST THROUGH THIRD GRADES

Growing up in Oakland public schools was quite an education. First grade was okay, but I was only there for half the school year. We played on monkey bars just like kids at any other school, and, boy, did I like the bars. We did all kinds of tricks such as the lemon drop, dead man's drop, the cherry drop, and swinging without any hands, going around and around. I always wanted to join gymnastics, but that was as close as I ever got to it. Apparently, my family was always on the borderline of being poor. Or at least that's how my mom made it seem. Therefore, extracurricular activities that cost lots of money were a no go. Thank God, my mom thought horseback riding lessons were inexpensive.

Second grade was a little different. I was tested for being dyslexic, but they didn't know enough about it back then, so I passed. Meaning I didn't get any help. That year was also when I became aware of more fights. A lot of the fights occurred before or after school at Tim's doughnut shop where Edwards turns into 73rd Avenue in addition to our fair share of fights at school. If you had any lunch money, some of the kids would intimidate or fight you for it. If you had candy, they'd want to fight you for that, too. There was always a fight over something. I think there were a lot of angry kids there. I'll never forget that my Valentine's Day cards were stolen in my second-grade class.

By that time, I had really started to hate school and discovered that having a stomachache could buy me some time at home. Unfortunately, being sick at my house meant no phone, no friends, and no TV, so it was definitely a catch twenty-two.

Then the famous movie *Roots* came out and made my life even more miserable. It was an extremely graphic and horrible portrayal of the brutality of slavery. In those days, television shows weren't really graphic like they are now. It showed how evil the white man was to African Americans. I couldn't believe that humans could treat other humans so cruelly, just because they had a different skin color. I got as far as when Kunta got whipped for not acknowledging his given slave name, Toby. I was horrified. I never watched the whole movie, because it was so horrifying. Let me just say that I have never been a racist and do not promote such behavior. But that movie got me into a lot of fights. I've definitely been on the receiving end of bigotry. I don't know how many times I've been called a "honky," and I've been told my mother and my father were involved in the slave trade. Remember, this was coming from some seriously angry children from school. My parents never displayed any prejudice in our home. Later in life, my parents helped a nice woman named Lilly from Nigeria, and I still consider her my sister. One day, Nicole, a few neighbor kids, and I were walking home from school, when two boys who didn't like my sister caught up to us and pulled a knife. Thank God for Rosie's cousin Chris, who drove up and scared the boys off.

Those days weren't all bad, though. There was a time when Isabella, another girl, and I would play Charlie's Angels, and that was fun. It was never that bad when my friends were around and not turning on me (which would happen occasionally). I think Isabella would get jealous at times. We were so close that she didn't like me getting too friendly with anyone else. Once neither of us wanted to go to school the next day, so, after her riding lesson, we thought it would be a good idea to bathe in poison oak. Apparently, I'm not allergic to poison oak, just everything else, but Isabella was terribly allergic, and thank God we didn't kill her. She puffed up like a blimp, and her eyes swelled shut. So she had to stay home and get better while I wound up at school all alone.

Third grade was a lot like second grade, but I had my little group that was starting to form: Greg, Terrell, Marcus, Isabella, Erica, and sometimes Kelly. I should clarify that was my group at school. I felt like I was leading a double life, because at home there were my friends that only wore dresses and prayed before every meal, not to mention the "country" living. And then I had my school friends that were the opposite—swearing, fighting, and was more of what I would call the "hood" living. Our teacher, Mrs. Conklin, was pretty nice. Her daughter was really good friends with Pamela Sue Martin, who played Nancy Drew in the seventies TV series, so that was pretty cool. But I hadn't been in her class long when I realized I was having a hard time seeing the board.

Oh, no! I thought. *This can't be happening to me. This is awful. Please make this not be true.* I knew the inevitable was coming. It was bad enough I lacked nice clothes, had ratty hair, and was white, but now . . . glasses. *Are you kidding me?*

Just shoot me now. Glasses were the worst, just what I needed to add to my self-esteem issues. I just wanted to fit in somewhere. It seemed all the odds were against me. I was already a big scaredy cat, and now I was giving the kids more ammunition by getting glasses. The only good thing was that I didn't have to get the stupid glasses until the last day of the third grade. I had all summer to get used to them.

It was amazing when I could actually see. I remember the first time I really looked at a tree and noticed the outline of each leaf. And they always taught you to get the license plate of a car that looked suspicious; I thought that was some kind of joke, but now I could read the license plates. I'd had no idea my eyesight was so bad until I could see clearly.

NEW KID IN TOWN

Around that time, a new girl named Martha moved to our neighborhood. She wore glasses, too. The house her family moved into had always attracted weird people. There was a lesbian couple that supposedly beat their dog. I say "supposedly" because people made all kinds of judgments on Holy Hill. Then there were some Hell's Angels, and, after Martha, some Buddhists, whom the church people called devil worshippers. If only I'd known then what I know now, wow! Martha was another white girl, a little chubby, and about our age. Her mom was really pretty, and Martha had a little sister named Claire. Martha also lived with her stepdad, who had the same vibe as Mr. Ellings, Darnell, and Sawyer. I couldn't put my finger on it, but he seemed very angry all the time. I thought he was downright creepy, but he ordinarily didn't interact with us at all. Once, Lyle and his friends, the troubled boys in the neighborhood, were driving extra fast around a dangerous corner, and Martha's stepdad went chasing after them with a wrench. Not to mention that Martha's stepdad had come home early from work and found me there at the house. Martha hadn't done all her chores yet, and he went ballistic. He started yelling, and then he kicked her and punched her. I had never seen a parent do that before. I thought he was going to hit me. That kick broke poor Martha's thumb.

Martha's stepfather never allowed her to bring home company but, when her parents were at work, we liked hanging out there. Unsupervised, we could eat as much sugary cereal as we wanted, make serious prank phone calls, and smoke cigarettes, which made us feel *really* cool. We would sit in the bathroom by the window, puffing on Martha's stepdad's cigarettes, blowing the smoke out the window, and feeling pretty tough. Afterwards, we'd take a Cling Free sheet and rub it all over ourselves to get the smoke out of our clothes. Once my mom caught us and asked if we had been smoking. Of course, I was freaking out inside, so I blamed one of the troubled boys in the neighborhood and said he had blown smoke in our faces.

THE BOYS IN THE HOOD

David and Lyle Costas were the troubled and rowdy boys who lived a couple of doors down from my house. They had a really bad reputation because their father wasn't around. Their mom, Polly, smoked a lot of cigarettes and drank quite a bit and definitely did not fit in as a Holy Hill church woman. Apparently, when David and Lyle's father lived with them, he used to beat them up pretty badly. I was convinced they had brain damage. They didn't do very well in school. David was very dyslexic and I believe that Lyle was too. So, back then, they put David in the special education class for severely handicapped children. That's not good for anyone's self-esteem. So people made fun of David and called him names that I'd rather not say. Anyway, it made for a very angry kid. David and Lyle got into a lot of trouble, and the cops were always chasing after them when they were older. But, on Holy Hill, it seemed as though it was always the girls against the boys.

One time, Lexi and I were riding our bikes on the hill. As I was pushing my bike up the steep part by Lexi's house, we ran into Sawyer and David, and David decided he was going to throw firecrackers at us. He was such a jerk, and I was frustrated because I had to get home. I was also afraid of getting blown up by them. They just laughed, and it pissed me off, but there wasn't anything that I could do, because there weren't any adults around. Lexi was kind enough to help me take my bike home, and we trekked through the backside of the hills. Of course that meant going through the woods and over an empty creek bed, which wasn't much fun. I was really mad at David for that, because he was so mean and scared me. I just wished he would go away.

So what do all kids do when somebody's mean to them? They take it out on other people. And some of us girls were so mean to the other boys on the street. Another couple of girls moved into the neighborhood, Dara and Dayna, who lived on Rifle Lane. We showed them how the girls act in our neighborhood. So, when Rudy and Chucky, the other not so rowdy boys, were around, we showed them how to beat them up. We also made up a little song where we called them Rudy the Booty and Chucky the Fucky. Looking back now, I feel really bad. Eventually, David hooked up with them, and then I didn't feel so bad. The story about Rudy and Chucky was that their mother was supposedly a hooker and worked at night to support her kids. Again, I don't know if that was true or not, but if you didn't go to church you were considered worldly and must have been up to all kinds of worldly sins.

Rudy and Chucky didn't live on the hill very long. And that's when Kim, Cahn, and Binh moved into Rudy and Chucky's old house. Their dad was white and their mom was Vietnamese. They had a cocker spaniel named Fluffy. I believe that the dad was Kim's stepdad and a Vietnam vet. He was a little strange, with a high-pitched voice that didn't fit his appearance. The parents never talked normally; they always yelled at each other. There seemed to be a lot of bruises and scars on the girls, much like Martha. I'm not sure if he beat them or sexually abused them, but something was definitely going on with those kids. They were always looking over their shoulder, like they were really defensive, waiting for something bad to happen. They had an emptiness or hopelessness about them. It seemed like that went on a lot on the hill: maybe sexual or physical abuse, but certainly mental abuse. Holy Hill had its beauty, but it seemed there was always a lot of chaos in our neighborhood.

Allie and Amber lived next door to me. I don't remember exactly when they moved in, but, when they did, of course, we had to go meet them. Their mom, Janet, was really pretty and reminded me of Cher, in a weird kind of way. Their dad was African American, and he was great. At Halloween, he'd hide out at the top of the stairs and jump out at us, spraying a fire extinguisher and wearing a crazy, scary mask. Oh, we loved it. They were a pretty normal family, one of the few that didn't seem so dysfunctional. Their family was the closest to what my home life was like, at least until Allie and Amber's parents split up.

After that, Janet got a little kooky. She was always napping. She would slur her words sometime and had wide mood swings, happy one moment and angry the next. Rumor had it that she was on tranquilizers or something. It could have been from the divorce or her job as a youth probation officer. As time went on, she seemed to become more and more of a nutcase. She had a duck or goose and let it roam around her yard, which would have been fine if she'd had it fenced in and didn't live next door to two dogs. When one of Lindsay's dogs killed the bird, she started blindly shooting her gun at the dog. Thank God, she missed, but she was shooting near a barn and by Lyle's and David's house. She could have killed the horse or the boys' mom. Plus, I could hear her bellowing cries and screams from my bedroom with the window shut. I felt bad about the animal being killed and all, but I blamed Janet, not the dog. Ultimately, though, her behavior just added to the collective quirkiness of the people who lived on that hill.

Then there was Margie. Her family didn't belong to the

church. She lived near the Joneses on the other side of my street. All the kids knew that her house had a swimming pool in the backyard, so we had to find a way to meet her. And it didn't take long.

One day, Lexi and I were hanging around Martha's house waiting for her to come out and play, when Margie's mom drove by and told us that she had a daughter and we should come visit sometime. That day probably came sooner than she wanted, because we showed up at the door wanting to go swimming. So bold, I'll tell you. Margie and I became such good friends. Her family seemed very normal. Not! Her dad was a firefighter, but supposedly, he had a little drug business on the side. I never saw anything abnormal going on in the house, but whenever I hung out there, all the kids had to stay in the back room while the adults were there, and I heard from Martha that she had heard from her parents that Margie's dad was a drug dealer. As I got older, I put two and two together. It was just another example of the weird shenanigans in the neighborhood.

So, I think I've introduced you to the kids of Holy Hill and some of their dysfunctions, as well as the kids at school. We had a lot of interesting times. Although I had fun, there was always this uneasy feeling that there was something more than met the eye. The hill kids were sweet, but a little weird; the school kids were a bit rowdy, but I had to find a way to fit in, somehow. After all, this was my new environment.

ANGRY CHILDREN

Throughout those years, Isabella continued to be my best friend at school. We got up to all kinds of mischief together. Whenever I spent the night at her house, she and I would try to stay up all night. We'd sneak out of the house in our high-heeled shoes and play two square on the street. We thought we were pretty cool. We'd hide in the bushes when a car came by. We had great imaginations then; we'd have yarn and play like it was taffy, by wrapping it around bike wheels and pretending we were stretching the taffy, like you'd see at the Santa Cruz Beach Boardwalk. But then there were the not-so-innocent games. We'd play daycare, and you would not want our daycare ever watching your kids. We would beat them, especially Mrs. Beasley. She was my doll, and not a very attractive doll, so when she misbehaved, boy, she'd get it good. It was sad how we would beat our dolls, especially if they weren't pretty. Mrs. Beasley wore glasses and had short boyish hair. Her clothing wasn't very stylish either.

Our school endorsed violence, too. No one ever really got in trouble for fighting—maybe there were just too many fights to keep up with—but any student caught mouthing off was at risk of getting a spanking. You'd go to the book room, where the teacher or principal would take this big paddle with holes and hit you with it. Thank God I never got that. I was a pretty good student and never mouthed off, but my fourth-grade classroom was right across the hall from the book room, and I could hear all the screaming and crying that came from there.

Other than that, I liked my fourth-grade class. Miss Hill

was our teacher. She was nice, except if we didn't line up in an orderly fashion after the bell rang, we'd have to write stupid sentences saying, "I will line up orderly and quietly when the bell rings before class." I swear that's all we did. I believe fourth grade was when you were supposed to learn about the history of California, but I can assure you we did not. I knew nothing of missions or the pony express. And, Lord knows, our field trips were going to the BART station, a fire house, the park, or to see a play at another school. That's Oakland public schools for you. I should have known that this grade would be tainted. I got a serious migraine the first day of school and threw up in the office. I don't think I've ever had a migraine since that day. Something told me that this year would probably be significant.

DON'T BE A MARK

I was handling school okay by this time and trying to get good grades. Isabella and I would talk on the phone for hours doing homework, as we both were overachievers. She was really smart, and I was a good runner up, but I had this dyslexic problem, so I was a little slower. I seemed to be keeping my enemies at bay, so that was a relief. But the violence was still around. Like with Isabella's stepdad, Darnell, who I would learn much later in life, was a physically abusive man. When he was around thirty-six years old, he just dropped dead from a heart attack. That was pretty devastating for Vicki and Isabella, but he'd always scared me, so there was no love lost for me. And right around the same time, this poor girl got a phone call in our class that her father had died. Then at one point, this other girl's mom was shot in the head. I believe she lived, though.

The fighting continued at school, and by this time my sister had graduated from sixth grade and was going to Castro Valley schools. My mom didn't want my sister to go to King Estates Junior High because, at that time, the school was really rowdy, and Rosie had been jumped by some boys after school who'd bloodied her lip. Since my sister liked to fight and had quite a reputation after taking down one of the biggest school bullies, my mom thought it best she not go and get into any more trouble. Even she and I would fight like cats and dogs. She was always taller and bigger, so I'd never win. I couldn't wait to grow so I would finally be able to kick her ass.

As much as my sister and I fought, she wouldn't let anyone harm me. That was only for her to do and no one else.

LaVonne was my nemesis. She was small, but she had a big mouth and acted real tough. I was actually scared of her. I was taller, but I was a pretty skinny kid. What I didn't realize was that I may have been skinny, but I was always around horses and lifting heavy things, so I was pretty strong. Kelly and LaVonne were hanging out together, which I knew couldn't be good. Kelly had been part of our group, but she had kind of a ghetto mentality and sometimes she seemed really messed up. I was scared of her, too. She tried to make me give her my candy once, and I think I might have. She was known for hitting hard, but may have been just a rumor. Needless to say, I didn't want to find out the hard way. Then LaVonne came up to me hostilely and said, "Kelly said you was talking smack 'bout me!"

Which of course I was not. I was scared to death. But I kept remembering Larissa saying, "Don't be a mark." Back then—and maybe today, I'm not sure—when you were about to exchange blows, you did this cock fighting, shoulder bump thing. LaVonne would get her arms and fists going like she was playing an air guitar. It looked so stupid. Next, she was in my face with her finger pointing at me and yelling, "You was talking shit, and I'm gonna kick yo' ass." Such lovely language for fourth graders. Most of them sounded like truck drivers by the second grade, just trying to be cool. I pushed her hand out of my face, but then I started to cry. And you know what that meant? More ammo for LaVonne. "You scared? Look at you, crybaby," she said, her finger back in my face.

I was actually starting to get mad mixed with scared. Not a good combination, at least not for LaVonne. Apparently, I need my personal space, and she was really in my face, so I had to get her away. Finally, I'd had enough, and I pushed her so hard that she flew across the playground and landed on her ass. I even shocked myself. I didn't know I had it in me. Everything changed from that point on. There are always tons of people around when a fight breaks out, and as I wasn't very tough, the kids thought this was going down fast. It didn't turn out as they'd imagined, though. It felt so good to fling her across the playground. After that moment she changed her tune. "Uh, it wasn't you; I mean, uh, it was Kelly."

"No, it wasn't. You're the one startin' this mess. Shut yo' mouth before I kick yo' ass, bitch!" Boy, let me tell you, I turned into a whole new person with an attitude. People looked at me in a different way after that, even Isabella. I'd always thought the ones with big mouths were the toughest ones, but I was wrong. I didn't have a big mouth because I didn't want anyone calling my bluff. Isabella always had a big mouth and was quite witty when we had what we called "ranking" contests. (You would cap on each other or, in other words, talk about each other's mama.) All my friends were better at that than I was. I guess I would get so frustrated that I just started flinging my fists. It was like I had this breaking point, and then *snap!*

Martha found that out the hard way. We were doing the ranking game, but it got out of hand, and my glasses fell off and broke. Not okay, because my mom didn't want to have to pay for glasses, so now I needed the trouble I was about to get into to be worth my while. I was rewarded with the discovery that I was quite a fighter, and very strong. Martha was bigger than me and used to getting her ass kicked by her stepfather, but I had a lot of pent-up anger myself (I should have had a clue from beating on my baby dolls), and having the courage to face my fears head on gave me some serious confidence. When you're facing the humiliation of being pushed into a corner and feel like you can't do anything about it, you learn quickly to stand up for yourself.

After that incident, I finally gained some respect at school. Who would have thought that one little fight could have such a strong influence in my life? It totally changed me. I was no longer afraid; in fact, I went to the opposite extreme and became a bully. It seems to be a common phenomenon that bullies are actually sad and fearful people who were once bullied by someone else. Thank God I didn't stay in that phase for very long, but, at that time, I would get in anyone's face. There were a few boys who wound up on the receiving end because it was practice for me to keep up my fighting skills. I was always smart about it, though. I wouldn't get myself into confrontations unless they were one on one.

One day, Martha, Margie, and I were leaving school when we noticed some boys from another school who were looking at us strangely. We wanted to go home, so they were not about to deter us. This wasn't the first time these boys had come by. Someone said they went to Parker Elementary, which really is in the hood, somewhere between 82nd Avenue and somewhere not good. This was the first time they had followed us all the way to Martha's house. Well, Martha's nasty stepdad had this gun hidden under his bed, which was stupid. Kids *always* know where the guns are hidden. You can see this isn't heading down the best road. He was probably too stoned to know where he'd put it. We had found it at an earlier time, hidden under his bed, so we thought, *We'll take care of these boys.* We ran and got the gun, cocked it, pointed at them and said, "You'd better get your ass away from us before you get shot!" Let me tell you, they *ran.* As any self-preserving person would. They never followed us crazy white girls again. We were starting to earn that reputation honestly. The bad thing was the gun stayed cocked and we didn't know what do, so, after playing with it for a while, we put it back under the bed. How lucky we were to not have killed those boys or one of us? We've all heard the tragic stories before. There must have been divine intervention.

CRAZY WHITE GIRLS

Word must have got out at school, because we were now known as "the crazy white girls" on the hill, and I liked that reputation. I felt safe and strong and figured no one would mess with me. I was starting to lose my fear. I was no longer afraid of dogs—well, most of them—and I wasn't afraid of the school kids anymore. I realized that I wasn't that much different from them. I started to back off from being a bully, because that wasn't really who I was, but I still wouldn't hesitate to stand up for an underdog.

After the whole LaVonne thing went down, Isabella and I got even closer. That's also the time I realized she wasn't as tough as she made herself out to be. This stupid white boy, Adam, was picking on her on her way home from school, and she was getting upset, so guess who came to save the day? The little scaredy cat who discovered she wasn't takin' no shit from anybody got all up in his face, and I think I punched him. Isabella may have deserved whatever he was dishing, but not on my watch. As close as she and I were, we were about to get even closer.

After grieving Darnell, Vicki met someone at her work, a nurse named Robert. It was weird for a guy to be a nurse back then, but whatever. Vicki was so nervous about their first date, but she and Robert turned out to be a match made in heaven. He came to my house to pick Vicki up for their first date. My mom helped get her get ready and Isabella was spending the night, and I liked him right away. He was a real hippie, with the best energy, an all-around great guy—not like a lot of the other dads I had encountered. And the more we all hung out, the more he could see how Isabella treated me. I could tell he thought she was a brat sometimes, and I liked having someone on my side of the court. Once, we were on a three-week vacation, and Isabella was being cold and acting like she was mad at me. Usually I would be the one to try to smooth things out, but I'd had enough of her attitude, and I saw Robert watching this whole incident unfold. I asked Isabella, "What's wrong? Are you mad at me for something?" She didn't respond, just ignored me. Finally, in a stern voice I said, "Why are you acting like a spoiled brat? I'm sick of how you just give me the cold shoulder for no reason, tryin' to make me feel bad. Well, it ain't workin' this time. We can get along or not. It's up to you."

As all this was going down, I saw Robert's face as he gave me an "it's okay" smirk, as if to say, "Good for you." Finally, someone had seen what was happening, and it felt good. It seemed like most parents ignored their kids' bad behavior and would never stop them from doing it. I never really felt like anyone was on my side, except when I prayed to God. I believe that he kept me safe, at least as long as I followed the rules. Vicki, Robert, and Isabella were my other family. I was there all the time, and it was nice, because they wanted me there. They taught me more than they ever knew. They exposed me to so many different things that I would never have seen or experienced with my own family: baseball and basketball games, concerts, movies, renaissance fairs, and camping trips.

Around the time I started staying at their house a lot, HBO came out. Watching R-rated movies without commercials was a whole new experience for me, and it was exciting at first but eventually problematic, because I had a love-hate relationship with scary movies. I always thought I wanted to watch them, but they gave me nightmares. I was mostly scared of the satanic-type movies or anything supernatural. No one could prove to me that possession by the devil wasn't real, and I wasn't having any part of it.

My mom always knew how much certain movies scared me, so she was good about not letting me see them, until I stayed over at Isabella's and we watched the scariest movie of all times, *The Exorcist.* I still don't even like seeing the word here in this book. I usually refer it as the "E" movie. That is still the scariest movie ever. I had to tell my mom before we watched the movie so I wouldn't get Vicki or Robert in trouble, so my mom thought she'd teach me a lesson and let me see it. I was scared for a solid year. I couldn't sleep for about a week and couldn't have the lights off anywhere or anytime. Boy, did she teach me a horrible lesson.

It wasn't long after Robert and Vicki were together, maybe a couple of years or so, when Vicki got pregnant. We went on this amazing three-week road trip while she was pregnant. Things were a lot different in 1980. I remember their tan-and-brown VW bus. Robert and Vicki had a cooler of beer between their bucket seats, and were drinking from it the whole time. Vicki eventually had the baby, and he was the cutest thing you had ever seen.

His life was tragically cut short in the summer of 1981 before his first birthday. Isabella had been in Minnesota for her annual summer trip, when one of the cats knocked something into the floor furnace and set the house on fire. Vicki and Robert had been downstairs asleep and woke up to what seemed like small flames. Smoke travels up, and the baby's room was upstairs. The flames quickly consumed the house. When Robert tried to break through the window to save his baby, he got third-degree burns on his hands. The firefighters grabbed him to stop him, but it was too late. I remember watching Robert sobbing uncontrollably on the news. That was my first real experience with a death that affected me so deeply. And God was the only thing that could comfort me. If Isabella had been home, she would have died also. Too much violence and tragedy were going on all around my life. I needed solace. I found church.

Chapter 3

CHURCH

School was weird, but more like street-smart weird, rough and tough, while my neighborhood was just plain wackadoodle. Most of Holy Hill's residents belonged to the same church. They were Apostolic Pentecostals, which in layman's terms meant they were Holy Rollers. The girls all had to wear dresses, couldn't cut their hair, and makeup was seriously frowned upon; Lord knows you wouldn't want to look like a harlot or Jezebel. They totally stood out from everyone else. You definitely wanted to blend in at school, so as not to attract any unwanted attention. I was friends with these people, and I enjoyed hanging out with them at home, but school was different. I didn't want to be associated with them, because they were weird and got picked on. One time a boy told Lexi she had freckles because a cow had farted in her face. Who comes up with this stuff? Kids can be so cruel.

Pretty much the whole hill went to this church—and when I say, "went," I mean they went four times a week: Wednesday night, Friday night, and twice on Sundays, morning and evening. Friday night was when children's church happened. One day, Lexi's family invited me to go to children's church, and, social butterfly that I was, I would go anywhere just to get away out of the house. When we got there, Sister Jones was in charge and ran the group while her daughter Deanna played the slide guitar for us to sing hymns. The first scripture we learned was the Lord's Prayer. My mom got wind of it and said I had to learn the Catholic version and not the King James Version. She thought the church was some kind of cult, but she still let me go. I didn't know the difference then, but there are all kinds of versions of the Lord's Prayer, and I'm not here to tell you which one is right.

After children's church, the kids went out to the big church to listen to the sermon. How unbelievably boring, especially for a not-quite-seven-year-old. The main pastor was Brother Jackson and next in line was Brother Williamson. Other members would get up and speak, but they were never women, only men. They quoted a lot of scripture, and that old-fashioned language was hard to understand. They also followed a man they believed was a prophet, Brother Gilbert. So we listened to some of his old tape recordings instead of a live person. Once the sermon was over, everyone would get up and sing; that part was fun.

Then they would get to the testimony part, the praying and worshipping. That was weird and a little scary. They didn't do it right away, but, after I'd been to church a few times, they would let loose. It was like they were in a trance, a kind of meditative state. People were falling on the floor, crying, and sometimes screaming. Some of the words weren't even real words; they called it "speaking in tongues." They also danced around. That kind of dancing was okay because it was dancing for the Lord. You just couldn't do regular dancing in public. I found out later that dancing is not allowed because it is considered too suggestive and would make boys and men think nasty thoughts. Women were always blamed for making men think sinful thoughts. That was also the reasoning for why they had to wear skirts; if you had pants on, then a man could see everything and again have nasty thoughts. Women apparently had a lot of power, for second-class citizens.

Even though the church was very different from what I was used to, I found some comfort in it. After the sermon and worshipping was over, all the people in the church would shake my hand and say, "How are you, Sister Leah? I'm so happy to see you. I love your dress." Everyone would gather around in the babysitting room, which was in the back of the church, to make some kind of plan to hang out. Sometimes, you'd get to go out for ice cream or donuts. That was my favorite part of church, by far.

GETTING SUCKED IN

The church people were weird, but nice. I kept my church friends very separate from my school friends, because I cared what people thought. They didn't have TVs, the women and men had to dress and look a certain way, and no one was to swear. There was no alcohol, definitely no drugs, no cigarettes, and lots of other rules.

The church didn't have a huge congregation, but they loved to get new members. They even had some members spread throughout Canada, Mexico, Arizona, Indiana, and

Minnesota. And like a lot of churches, this one had a few ex-convicts. We had our share of needy people as well as helpers. Even though I was a needy child, I would have been considered one of the helpers, because I was quite the people pleaser.

Mother became concerned about my going to church when I started asking if I could on other days as well. To me it made sense, because I was an all-or-nothing kind of person; my motto is "go big or go home." But to my mom, it was a red flag. After all, she was a psychology major and had been raised Catholic.

Of course, I wanted to "save" my parents, like any newcomer or "born again." Usually the newbies want to fix the world. So I was just doing what I thought was right. I started asking her, "Mom, do you even believe in God? What about Dad? You probably should, or you might not go to heaven. Why can't I go to church more? It's a good thing. Don't you want me to do good?"

"Don't worry about me or your father," she said. "I think you're going too much to this church. You don't need to go more than once a week. The only reason they have their members go so often is to brainwash them. You can go once a week or not at all."

You know how persistent kids can be, well I was, "But why?" I believe I started to piss her off, so she ignored me. She probably was right about the brainwashing part, but I loved going. After all, I was told by Brother Jackson that I was a peacemaker and had the gift of discernment. *I have gifts?* I thought this was very cool.

The church had a lot of rules and pretty strict doctrine.

In fact, Lexi got the most beatings for asking too many questions and being rebellious. You weren't supposed to question anything. That's what having faith was all about. You were to always do what the Bible said, and, since there's a verse about never sparing the rod, when a child misbehaved, whether yours or someone else's, the adult would *not* be disrespected and therefore the child would get spanked. That was very apparent in the babysitting room at church and in the home.

At Lexi's house, we terrorized this one poor kid who was being babysat by Lexi's mom. If that kid didn't listen to us, well, he got it. That's probably why as an adult, I never wanted my children to be in an environment with a bunch of other kids that weren't being properly supervised. Mind you, he was probably only two or three years old, but if he didn't do as we said, he'd get it. We were so young and so angry. Obviously, we didn't know better, but I feel so guilty to this day. If his mother had been aware of what was going on, someone would have been arrested in today's world. But we were just acting out what we saw, and we were only seven or eight years old ourselves. That's how it was, though. You were always supposed to obey your elders. I was even told that I could hit Lexi because I was her elder.

Things started to get a little uneasy in the church when some of the members like the Joneses started to listen to a different doctrine from one of the other branches. There was a lot of talk of the Arizona church being against Brother Jackson's teachings, but it was only rumor at this point. The church was getting new members from other, more what we considered, backward states like Alabama. - *Funny, coming from a backwards hill.* - As the new members came, the divi-

sion of the elders was becoming more apparent; Brother
Jackson and Brother Williamson on one side, while Alabama
started to team up with the Joneses and Arizona people. One
such man, Achim from Alabama, was a bit violent. The violence didn't rear its ugly face until after he married one of the
head pastors, Brother Williamson's daughters, Annie. Achim
would photograph her in compromising positions, and then
he would show the pictures to his father. Allegedly, he physically abused her if she didn't consent. Eventually, Annie told
him she wanted a divorce, and Achim didn't handle that very
well; in his eyes, and in the church's eyes, once you got married, that was it. It was for life. Annie's father was not in fa-
vor of divorce, but under these circumstances it was allowed.

The division in the church between the elders was becoming more and more obvious and clear that there needed
to be a separation. Brother Jones and his family were in a full
fledge fight against Brother Jackson and Brother Williamson.
It was at this time that the Joneses took in Achim after his
marriage ended with Annie. On one church day, Achim tried
to break down the doors while church was in session, so he
could kidnap her. He screamed, "Where is my wife? I'm
gonna get you if it's the last thing I do! You belong to me,
Annie!" She went into hiding. She snuck out another door or
something. It seemed like she was always in hiding. Her
brothers were big young men and kept Achim out of the
church. Not to mention one of her brothers had his own personal complications with the Joneses.

One of the Joneses' daughters, Rhoda, married one of
Brother Williamson's sons, Curtis, and that only increased
the weirdness. Then Rhoda became nutty herself. There was

a rumor that she had hovered over her sleeping husband in the middle of the night with a big butcher knife and tried to stab him, but it was never confirmed.

After that, they too, got a divorce. In a church like this one, divorce was forbidden, but it was still happening. The church tried to discourage it by enforcing certain rules that made an example of anyone who divorced. Women weren't allowed to remarry, and divorced men could remarry but were forbidden to preach from the pulpit.

As much as the Joneses portrayed having it all—the perfect family, the nicest home, beautiful kids—apparently, that wasn't true. They had their own agenda. Once they started wanting to follow a doctrine other than what the Williamsons and the Jacksons were teaching—not to mention the two divorces—Sister Jones's daughter Deanna started to act very strangely indeed.

Deanna was the rebellious one in her family and the whistleblower. She didn't want any part of following the new doctrines her parents were teaching. She had been an integral part of the church for years, including helping her mother with the children's church. At age twenty-eight or so, she had spent her whole life living a certain way. But the church was changing, and she didn't want any part of it. She wouldn't keep her mouth shut about her opinions.

Once she told the brethren that her mother was standing up to her father, which was strictly forbidden, as men were supposed to be in control of their households. Her parents didn't want her telling anything that went on in their house. After all, she wasn't being a typical submissive woman. Women weren't supposed to have opinions; opinions were exclusively for men. To retaliate, the Joneses started making her out to be crazy, and it wasn't hard to believe, because her actions were indeed crazy. One day, she ran to Lexi's house. Lexi, who was only eleven years old at the time, answered the door and found a hysterical Deanna begging, "You have to help me. Please hide me. They're trying to kill me!"

Lexi was too young to know what to do; besides, all the church members had been told not to communicate with the Joneses, because they were now the enemy. Lexi wanted to help, but Rosie, who always followed the rules, intervened at the last minute and sent Deanna away. So Deanna ran down the street to the house of another neighbor who wasn't a member of this particular church, and ran right through their patio glass door. She cut herself up a bit, nothing requiring hospitalization, but that was all the talk for a bit. No one could figure it out.

Only a few weeks after that, we heard sirens and saw the ambulance come uphill, turn right, and go directly to the Joneses' house. I was at Margie's house, which was right next door, and everyone was freaking out. I said, "Margie, what's going on? It looks like an ambulance at the Joneses'." A few moments later, we saw the EMTs carrying a covered gurney out of the house and realized that Deanna must be dead.

I remember Sister Jones telling Margie's mom that Deanna had committed suicide—another unforgivable sin, according to the church—by taking a bunch of pills. "Deanna had been acting so strange lately," Sister Jones said. "We saw the empty pill bottle by her bed, and she wouldn't wake up. I hope she's with the Lord."

Then the stories started coming out about what really

happened. One of Lindsay's neighbors was dating an Oakland police officer, and he told her, "Something ain't right here. You should get a copy of the coroner's report. That family is bad." Also, Lindsay had a vision that Deanna had died at the hands of Achim and Rhoda, and, since they had some violent history, it seemed feasible. This, of course, never came out. I did get a chance to see the coroner's report; Lindsay got a copy of it, as it was public. Deanna hadn't died from an overdose at all. In fact, she had been in a straitjacket and her death was caused by asphyxiation. I don't know how you could do that to yourself in a straitjacket. And why had they lied about her taking pills? The report had a lot of details that were pretty graphic and totally different from what people were saying. This still stumps me to this day. No one was ever arrested or charged. I know that some or all of them in that house knew what really happened, but would never tell.

That's when I realized just how crazy churches could get. As I grew older and became more observant, I started to see things more clearly. I was also getting more involved in the church. I knew that not all the members supported murder or wrongful death, and that there were some good people left.

Not long after Deanna's death, the Joneses left town and moved to Arizona. I had always admired their cute house, but now I was convinced it was haunted, because of the craziness that had gone on there. I still can't believe how I used to go there for children's church and have lunch. I guess that everything that has a light side also has a shadowy side. I just hadn't known how dark that shadow could be. That's when I understood what a hypocrite was. I believe it says in the Ten Commandments, "Thou shalt not kill."

—

When I was around thirteen years old, I got invited to go to convention. The church people always went to Colorado during the summer, and I used to take care of everyone's yards and animals when they were away. I actually made really good money. A lot of them would make a vacation out of it. They would drive to Estes Park for the weeklong convention, and then some would go camping afterwards for another week or so. It seemed like they were gone for about three weeks. It was very lonely in the neighborhood, since most of the neighborhood went to the church.

Now it was my turn to go, and I was so excited. I went with the Halls, and we had a blast caravanning. We stopped in Steamboat Springs around the Fourth of July. They had a rodeo, and, being horse people, of course we went. We did this for a few years in a row. One time, Lexi's younger sister Ellen, who was always accident-prone, happened to walk behind one of the horses and got kicked. She wound up with a huge horseshoe print on her stomach.

We finally got to the actual convention and everyone was there, from all over—Canada, Indiana, Illinois, Minnesota, and many other states. Everyone was so friendly and accepting. One of the sermons that stood out was on the difference between grace and legalism. The preacher talked about Jacob being tricked into marrying Leah, when he thought he was marrying Rachel. Leah was the representation of legalism and disgrace: doing something because you are told to do it, not because it is truly in your heart or through grace. This sermon was extremely relevant to me, as I was noticing more and more hypocrisy. Of course, everyone looked back at me to see how I was responding, or they smirked, since my name is Leah. My darling sister decided to tie the belt of my skirt to the pew, so when I stood up, I got yanked back onto the bench. Nothing like drawing extra attention to myself. I was mortified, needless to say. Everyone hung out after the service to chat. When Brother Barrot, who had given the sermon, came up to me and introduced himself, it was very awkward when I told him my name was Leah.

Church had all these great values and ideas, but the stuff that really went on was just plain nuts. They considered everyone in the church to be saints, but, let me tell you, most of them were the farthest thing from a saint. They acted very holier-than-thou, but I was always shocked or disappointed when the truth came out. The greed and the physical and sexual abuse were absolutely insane. I know this happens all over the world, but I guess it seems worse when you profess to be chosen by God.

The church was run by men, and women were never allowed at the pulpit. They were treated like second-class citizens. If a woman spoke against her husband, the church would always take the man's side. Most of the members were discouraged from going to college, because they might become too "worldly." That would be detrimental to the church. If the church people really knew what was really going on in the world, or saw the way others lived, they might choose to leave the church. The membership would dwindle and so would the cash flow. Of course, the church helped a lot of their members, and, unfortunately, some people just took advantage. Some turned a blind eye to what was going on just in case they, too, needed help from the church.

Politics played a big part in the church as well. Everyone turned a blind eye to activities that involved certain members. I was hanging out with Lindsay quite a bit by now, and she was really close with Brother Jackson. So I was spending a lot of time at the Jacksons too. I became very close with the head pastor, and had many talks and dinners over there.

I always liked going to the Jacksons' house. They seemed like the real deal. They had their problems but didn't try to hide them. They had a daughter and a son who left the church to find themselves and another son who was a heroin addict. And they didn't shun their kids. So as I got closer, I started to question some of the people's behaviors. I would bring certain situations up to Lindsay, and then we would go together to Brother Jackson to discuss them. Lindsay always had the reputation for being one to stir up the pot; now, I was getting to be known for that, too.

I was hanging out at Lindsay's all the time. She had moved to the Hawk Man's house, so called because the man who had lived there before her had all kinds of birds. He would walk the streets with a hawk on his shoulder, and he had a huge harpy eagle named Monique. Rumor had it that if she was out flying, people should keep their babies and small children inside. That seemed a little extreme, but, let's face it, there were quite a few extremes on the hill.

I had what Brother Jackson would call "the gift of discernment," so I was aware of many things going on in the neighborhood, whether or not they were made public. I can read people and situations very well. I didn't always know the gory details, but had my suspicions. There was generally an undercurrent of sex and violence at the Halls' house. The violent part was covered up by calling it discipline. Poor Lexi was beaten frequently. I remember her screaming bloody murder, being chased up the stairs by her laughing father, who had a belt in his hand. Somehow, I think he took great pleasure in terrorizing her. I always had thought she was just being dramatic and looking for attention.

One time I was at Lexi's first house, and there was a fly underneath Claire's crib. Now this room had four girls sleeping in it; there was a bunk, a pull-out bed, and a crib. So Lexi and I were trying to kill this fly and in walked Lexi's mom. We were under the crib on the floor, and Lexi was wearing a dress, which is not very practical for a kid climbing all around, and it had hiked up in the back. Lexi's mom said sternly, "What are you girls doing?" She implied there was some funny business going on.

Lexi answered, "Killing a fly."

Lexi's mom looked at me and said, "I think you need to go home. This behavior is unacceptable. Lexi can't play with you anymore."

I was mortified! I knew what she was thinking. And that was so *not* what was going on. I felt so bad and so wrong. There was funny business going on in her house right under her nose, but it wasn't me doing inappropriate things to Lexi; it was her own flesh and blood—her precious, holier-than-thou prince of a son, Sawyer. It all came out later in life that Lexi's brother had been sexually abusing her since she was five years old. Back then, I was too young to know what that meant, but I had an idea it was dirty. It wasn't until later that all the dirt would surface. Just like when you washed a carpet and it looked all pretty and clean at first, then the dirt would start to show up again. No wonder Lexi was such a drama queen—she was simply trying to let everyone know that something was terribly wrong. But when they belong to a church with such strong doctrines, some people will do whatever it takes to cover up any evil or wrongdoing. After all, they shut Deanna up permanently.

It seemed to me the more holy one professes to be, the shadier one truly is. It's sad to feel that way, but as you can see, this was my reality. There was murder and now incest. Church was supposed to be where I found peace, love, and acceptance, but more and more crazy stuff kept happening.

Nora was one of the Ramos girls from southern California. Nora's dad was a car salesman, so they always had fancy cars. Sawyer was really into Nora; it was as if they were betrothed or something. She was only ten years old when this was all being planned out, and I believe Sawyer was in his mid-teens. This was perfectly acceptable in the church's eye. As we all got older, Sawyer wasn't the mean, awful brother to Lexi anymore and Sawyer and I became friends which came in handy for him. Sawyer and Nora sent love letters to each other all the time, but they needed to be discreet; that's where Nicole and I came in as messengers. We sure used the bathroom a lot. I would go in and hide a letter there, and Sawyer would retrieve it and leave a letter for me to send to Nora. Sometimes Sawyer and I would meet to have these in-depth conversations about their relationship. I liked meeting with him because he was cute and I was pretty homely, and I liked male attention however I could get it. I felt special keeping this hidden and all. I had no idea what Sawyer was really all about.

As their relationship progressed and they got older, Sawyer made the mistake of telling Nora how much he had missed her and that, out of loneliness, he turned to his Malamute dog. And I don't mean in the sense of "man's best friend," but in a very twisted way. The dog soon disappeared and was never to be seen again. When Nora told Lindsay and me what he had done to the dog, we of course, told the church elders. Then we found out that the elders made Sawyer shoot his dog as punishment for his disgusting behavior.

When I look back at all this crazy stuff, I see that sexual and violent undertones were all over that hill. Everyone was so proper, nice, helpful, and caring, but you knew something was going on; you just didn't know exactly what. There was a whole secret life going on in this holy place. As in the book, *The Dark Side of the Light Chasers*, there is always a shadowy side for every light side; that's what makes one whole.

I always thought something was off with Lexi's dad, so I didn't realize it was her brother. Rosie was upset and didn't know how to deal with this particular situation she had observed. She said that she had gone down to the basement and walked in on Sawyer and Ellen in a sleeping bag. She didn't really see anything, but she thought it wasn't normal, so she brought it up to Lindsay, and, of course, that got the ball rolling about their family. There was a big meeting about the whole situation, and I was there to point out how Sawyer got away with so many things that others did not.

Before all this sick, twisted stuff about Sawyer came out, I didn't think he was that bad. I, too, was having a forbidden love affair. I was sneaking around with an older man, and when I got caught the outcome was very different. But I'm getting ahead of myself.

Chapter 4

BOYFRIENDS

I started to come into my own as far as looks go in the eighth grade. My teeth weren't so prominent anymore, I got a cool haircut—the eighties feathered style—and I got a new pair of glasses that were much more attractive. My skin wasn't as broken out as it had been when I first hit puberty. Boys began paying attention to me, so that made me think that I was actually getting pretty. I got my first boyfriend at the end of eighth grade—another Sawyer, if you can believe it. He was in the seventh grade, but he was taller than I was and very cute.

There was a buzz around my friends that Sawyer was interested in me, and, since there was a dance coming up that he was going to be at, I had to go. We became boyfriend and girlfriend at that dance. Our relationship was pretty typical for junior high kids. We'd talk on the phone quite a bit, and he would walk me to every class. He was the first boy that I ever French kissed, and that was how he'd leave me at each class, with a kiss. We went to Great America, an amusement park, or we'd just hang out. That was pretty much the extent of it. He was very normal, not a church member, and things were very age appropriate. I did struggle with the fact that the church said I shouldn't have a boyfriend, especially since he wasn't in the church. I really didn't have strong feelings of love for him, even though I said the words. I remember him saying "I love you" on the phone when he was getting ready to hang up, and I didn't want to be rude by not saying it back. It felt so awkward. We were together for about a month, which is pretty long for junior high, until I ended it. So I continued to lead a double life. I had my worldly one and my church one, and I kept them separate.

I started to go to parties and loved the popular crowd that I was a part of. Junior high was a great time for me, unlike the rest of the world. I was going to school in Castro Valley at this point, which was much safer and less stressful. It was nice not worrying about whether I was going to get in a fight that day. I was getting good grades, I broke track records, and I had a ton of friends. I was a peer counselor, which meant I was called out of class in order to counsel some of my fellow students and got school credits for it. I don't know how good I was, but I seemed to know a lot of people's business. I was the one everyone came to with their relationship problems, even though I hadn't experienced any of my own yet. It was weird how everyone opened up about problems that actually didn't seem that bad, considering what was going on with all my friends on the hill. But I did the best I could, and I loved the fact that I was helping people and that they needed me.

At the beginning of summer after the eighth grade, I started hanging out at Lindsay's more and more. She had badminton, volleyball, or ping-pong set up in her front yard on a regular basis, and it was so much fun. She was twenty-seven by then and married with two children, and she always had guys over at her house. Since I was getting more attractive, I was learning how to be quite the flirt. One of the men who spent a lot of time at the house was Lindsay's brother-in-law, Sal. He was twenty-two when I met him, and he had just started going to the church. He was the new, hot, Mexican guy and looked like Chachi from *Happy Days*.

Sal was starting to show interest in me, and, oh yeah, I was very excited about that. Looking back, I know how wrong it was for a twenty-two-year-old to be romantically involved with a fourteen-year-old, but at the time I thought I was hot stuff. I really liked Sal; I was convinced I had found the guy I was supposed to marry, and I thought we would get married and play house. Then, I could be related to Lindsay, and she would really be my family. I was in total fantasyland. Isn't that what all young girls dream of?

I spent a lot of time at her house learning how to cook, clean, take care of the house, and drive. She showed me how to write checks and deposit slips—all the things I should have learned from my parents. I remember Lindsay telling me to do something and I asked her a thousand questions so I wouldn't do it wrong. I was used to an OCD mother, and if the dishwasher wasn't loaded properly—and when I say properly, I mean the way my mom wanted it—you'd hear about it. My mother was a micromanager. There was only one right way to do things, and she knew what that was. Lindsay was totally different. She told me to figure it out and reassured me that it would be fine, but you can understand why I asked so many questions: I didn't want to be wrong again. I wanted to learn all these new things that would make me a good wife.

Church on Friday nights was becoming more fun, because all the young adults would go out afterwards, and we got to ride in the guys' cars. And you know that all teenage girls want to do at that age is to be around boys. All the guys were older than us, already out of high school, and we were just finishing up junior high. There weren't many male church members our age. Besides, the church's rules about females obeying their elders and their men meant that young girls were often encouraged to be with older men. After all, the head pastor was thirty-three years older than his wife. People didn't really worry about the age factor on Holy Hill.

I always hoped I could ride with Sal or at least get to sit next to him when we were out. Most of the time that was the case. When it was time to go home, I always got dropped off at Lindsay's, and then Sal would walk me home.

I'll never forget the first time we kissed. Talk about awkward. Sal actually told me I was kissing him the wrong way and he would show me how it was supposed to be done, since I was so naïve. I was young and had only kissed one boy, Sawyer, in eighth grade. I thought we had done it right. Things were moving fast with Sal, which I thought was much like Sawyer's and Nora's relationship (before theirs got all kinky and weird). Although I knew my parents probably wouldn't see eye to eye with me on the age thing, my after-church outings with Sal continued all summer long. It looked like I had a real boyfriend.

Once I started high school, Sal would meet me during school hours because I had off-campus lunch in Castro Valley.

That wasn't enough, though. He wanted to be with me more and more. I thought that was great, so I would let him sneak through my bedroom window. That went on for about a year or so. I don't know how we got away with it for as long as we did—and eventually, our little secret was made known.

One night—actually really early one morning—Lindsay's horse Dandy tried to get into the barn for some hay. Lindsay needed Sal's help and realized he was nowhere to be found. He had fallen asleep in my room, and boy was that scary, because I had to sneak him out of the house before my parents figured out that he had been there.

The phone rang that morning. I rushed to answer, and Lindsay was on the other end. She said, "I need to talk when you get home from school." That was the extent of the call, but my heart sank—I knew exactly what it meant. Sal had never stayed the night. *If only he hadn't fallen asleep, we would never have been caught,* I thought. I was a horrible liar, but I was pretty good at leaving things out. If somebody didn't ask the right questions, then I wouldn't have to lie, which made me feel better.

The day dragged, but school came to an end and it was time for the inevitable talk with Lindsay. Lindsay gave me that look of *I know what you've been doing* and said, "So, you've been having a visitor, haven't you?" She wanted to know exactly what had gone on at my house. "You know the brethren are going to want to know about this. What were you thinking? What if your mom found out? Do you know how this would look? She would never let you come to church again. You'd better tell me everything, and I mean everything."

Although Sal and I had never gone all the way, I was still

embarrassed to talk to her about our relationship. But I managed to say, with tears in my eyes, "You want me to tell you details? That's private. I don't feel comfortable telling you everything. Maybe you should ask Sal."

With that, she shifted tactics and started asking me specific questions, which were easier for me to answer. "So, did you have sex with him?"

"No," I said, which was so much easier than telling her everything straight up.

"Did he touch you?"

Quietly, with my head down so I wouldn't have to look her in the eye, I murmured, "Yes." She wanted to know where, so then I gave her all the details.

When I finished my explanation, she said, "You're gonna have to talk to the elders and explain yourself." Then she muttered, "Sal is in really big trouble." There was absolutely no way I could get out of this predicament. I would have to talk to the elders and confess my sins. I just felt sick to my stomach.

I'm not sure exactly what day I had the "meeting," but I do remember being taken into the room next to the pulpit. It was Brother Jackson and Brother Williamson, and they both wore very serious looks of concern. Which made me feel even worse. I was scared and felt very shameful. It started out with Brother Williamson saying, "Hum, well, what's going on with you? You know why we are here having this meeting, right? It's come to our attention that you and Sal have been spending time together, is this correct?"

I solemnly answered, "Yes."

Brother Jackson chimed in, "You see how this is a problem, don't you? Your mother could press charges against Sal, and it could come back to the church. What exactly is the nature of your relationship? Did you have sexual intercourse with Sal?"

"No, sir."

"Well, we need to know what did happen. There are certain ways you are allowed to have sexual relations, but some are forbidden. We don't want you sinning."

They both just stared at me. Somehow, I had to explain in graphic detail what had happened. Can you imagine how embarrassing that was? I was a teenager discussing my love life with these two grown men, which was pretty terrible. Of course, it was very important that I was still a virgin, but there still is a lot you can do without having intercourse. It seemed that as I was telling them things—and I hope I was wrong—they enjoyed the conversation. I really hope my feelings were wrong, because that is so unfair to use your spiritual authority like that. I'm pretty sure it was more to degrade me and make me feel so ashamed and guilty. Needless to say, Sal was excommunicated for a while and was not allowed to come to church on the days I was there as a punishment. I believed the elders talked to him, too, but I don't know what was said. That's when I started to see the favoritism in the church. Sawyer could be with Nora, but I couldn't be with Sal. What was the difference?

It wasn't until I was sixteen that I found out Sal had been hanging out at the Smoked Hollow where he'd fallen in love with a waitress who would soon become his wife. However, she was from Mexico and had married to get into the country, not for love. So, being the good Christian that I was, I agreed to accompany Lindsay to the INS office to try to find out where this marriage license was and to get Sal's girlfriend divorced. There was also a part of me that thought, deep down, that if Sal saw I was helping him, he would change his mind and see how great I really was. At the very least, it would be another adventure with Lindsay.

I'll never forget that day. I had left Castro Valley High School after the ninth grade and transferred to Skyline High School in Oakland. On this particular day in my junior year, Oakland public schools were on one of their many strikes, so we hadn't been in class since before Christmas break. On the morning of January 28, 1986, I was eating breakfast and watching TV, and it was the launch of the space shuttle *Challenger*. I wasn't exactly sure what I was watching, because something didn't look right. Oh, my God, it blew up! Right on national television, the *Challenger* blew up. I couldn't believe my eyes. All those people died instantly. It was unbelievably tragic.

I went to Lindsay's house still in shock over the *Challenger*, but we were off to San Francisco to the Immigration Bureau. For some reason, no one could find any documents on Sal's new fiancée or her sisters' documents. It turned out that some lawyer had ripped off Sal's fiancée and her sisters by taking their money for fake marriages and giving them fake green cards. Their whole family freaked out because most of them weren't here legally. She couldn't get a divorce because she technically wasn't married. I'm sure this sort of thing happens all the time, but I'd never known anyone is that kind of situation. This was the beginning of Lindsay and me becoming a sort of private investigation team. These events would push Sal's marriage into high gear.

I was such a trouper that I actually helped out quite a bit with Sal and his fiancée. I was very good at pretending to be a tough, strong individual. But it hurt, and it was just another rejection. I probably should have been used to this by then. On their wedding day, I wore a black and white dress and red high heels (not too high, due to church rules), and I was carrying some stuff to the car when, *bam*! I totally lost control going down the slippery wet stone path to the driveway. I still remember how much that hurt. I had a huge bruise on my bum. I tried not to cry, because isn't it funny when that sort of thing happens to someone else? *Not*! I had been in my third year of Spanish, so I was helping to interpret some of the wedding program. Probably not that well, but I tried. The best part, and maybe a little reciprocal karma, was during the reception at Lindsay's parents' house. They had a big house and yard to match, and all the church girls were getting the food and drinks prepared. We had made this delicious citrus juice that would go inside kegs. Well, apparently, you can't do that. The citric acid does something to the inside of the keg that creates a toxin. Everyone was getting sick and puking their guts out. It still makes me laugh, probably because I didn't get sick. Karma works in mysterious ways, and I'm privileged to see it often, probably because I'm not really hoping for it at the time.

Despite the humor in that moment, I was pretty sad for quite some time after the wedding. After all, the church had made Sal and me stop seeing each other. I had thought he would wait for me until I was eighteen. I should have known better, but I was too young and naïve. Although the church didn't see anything wrong with an age difference like ours,

Sal probably knew on some level that to the outside world he just looked like a pedophile, and so he did the right thing by breaking things off with me.

In hindsight, I realize that my experience with Sal was one example of my tendency to always search for the unattainable, at least when it came to relationships with guys. I usually managed to find some form of rejection in my more intimate relationships. I was terrified of sex because it was such a sin to do out of wedlock, so guys rejected me a lot, because they wanted sex, and there were other girls who would give it to them. That was not going to be me; in turn, I turned to drugs and alcohol.

Chapter 5

LET'S PARTY

I had worked since I was fourteen years old, but that was cleaning house and working in a horse, tack, and feed store. I had to support the horse I had bought when I was fourteen. I was fortunate to keep my horse at the Jacksons' house, which was free. I actually liked visiting with Brother Jackson, despite my embarrassing confession; plus, I had been so involved with the church. But that was all about to change.

In the summer of '86, I was seventeen years old, had bought a car, and was starting what I considered to be my first real job, waitressing in the coffee shop at the local Five and Dime. Somehow, this just felt different, maybe because it paid much more than I had been making. My sister was a waitress there, and I followed in her footsteps. The whole waitressing job was a little intimidating, but I seemed to catch on pretty quickly. One of my first tips was $10 on a $1.50 slice of pie.

Another perk of the job was that I met a new friend, Annie. She wasn't really nice to me at first, but, for some reason,

I often seemed to get along with difficult people. One day, she needed someone to cover her shift so she could go to a rock concert. I needed the money and the hours, so I offered to cover her shift, and that was the start of a new friendship.

Annie and I worked a lot of the same shifts until school started again, but in that short time I introduced her to some of my friends and she introduced me to some of her friends and some other things. We started partying quite a bit. My friends and I were mostly drinkers or potheads. I had gotten drunk for the first time, on scotch, when I was a camp counselor in the eighth grade, and I had gotten stoned on pot sometime around the same time. I didn't like pot very much, but I loved to drink. So I did that pretty regularly. Some of my friends did other drugs, but not in front of me because they knew that I didn't do them.

Annie's friends weren't exactly like my friends. You could say they were unique, just like Annie. Annie's mom, who was a cook at the Five and Dime, had been an alcoholic and a hardcore drug addict—heroin, speed, you name it—who didn't even have a house. They moved from motel to motel, one dive to another. Annie's father had passed out on the floor once with a needle in his arm, and Annie had found him there when she was little. He had ended up in prison and had died at some point. Annie and her brother Nick were taken away and put into foster care for a while until their mother got her act together enough to get them back. Annie used to say, "She should have left us there and we might have had a chance."

Believe it or not, I would never have thought of their mother that way, because when I met her at the Five and

Dime, she had been clean and sober for a year and stayed that way ever since. She worked her program all the time. I first heard about AA when Annie's mom got her chip for being one year clean and sober, which is a big milestone. When Annie's mom explained to me what AA was about, it reminded me a little of church. AA didn't use the term "God" specifically, it was "Higher Power" instead, and they had the twelve steps. It was their own set of rules, but you could break them and not be punished like when rules were broken in the church.

Since Annie's mom had spent years under the influence, Annie had a lot of freedom to roam when she was younger. And you know the saying: "While the cat's away, the mice will play." She certainly played and met all kinds of interesting characters. She also discovered speed, go fast, crystal meth, crank—whatever you wanted to call it. Looking back now, I realize that even though Annie didn't like her mom doing drugs, she was doing the exact same thing. I never gave it much thought at the time, because I was only seventeen, and I had my own opinions of what was okay, as far as drug use, and what was not. If you could still function in society while partying, then it must be okay, right? I knew I wasn't a drug addict or an alcoholic, and Annie surely didn't seem like one either. I was interested in getting to know Annie and in expanding my horizons and I was ready to experiment. Annie had told me what great fun speed was, and, though I was a little bit scared of drugs, at the same time I was very curious.

Annie and I went to the South Bay to one of her old hangouts and met up with one of her friends. Travis was considered to be one of the coolest guys there, and he took a liking to me. He was cool, and even though he wasn't that cute, I liked the attention. I knew that being new in town had its advantages. I think Annie just liked him because he knew "the source," how to get things. We drove down to the tubes by the water, a known spot in Brisbane, and that's where I discovered snorting drugs. I was afraid at first. I knew it was wrong, being illegal and all, and God wouldn't like it. You were supposed to treat your body like one of God's temples, and this was not treating your body like a temple, by any means. This was very harmful, and I knew better. But I figured God would forgive me because I was young and experimenting. Also, my desire to try things was a little bit stronger than my fear of God at that particular time. I wasn't sure what speed did, and I didn't want to lose control or hallucinate. (I'd had a bad experience with pot in my junior year and thought I would be the first person in the world to overdose on pot and die.) I soon found out that's not what happens when you do speed.

At first, I didn't really notice anything different, but it sure felt good. I had all this energy, and I was very interested in pretty much everything. This was much better than alcohol. Alcohol had always been a problem for me, and I should have known it, ever since I'd been given the nickname "Leah Pukia." Speed was so much fun, and I was in control. Or at least that's what I thought. Annie said my pupils would get big, and I should try not to look her mother in the eye at work because she would know. That didn't happen either. It also suppressed my appetite, double bonus. This was the drug for me. I was on a quest from that weekend on.

Every weekend, I would say I was spending the night at

Annie's and she was spending the night at my house. We weren't at either house; we'd be in the city or wherever all night. We definitely had much more freedom than most kids nowadays. We always made it on time for work, though. We were the good old reliable ones. In fact, I remember trying to call in sick once, and my boss got so mad that she hung up on me. Annie and I were really on top of things at the restaurant. We could run circles around some of the weekend crew, and the boss knew she'd have her hands full if we weren't there.

I was also meeting all kinds of new friends through work, and that included older friends who liked to party. Nancy, our assistant manager, was in her mid-twenties and already married with a kid. Since I had already spent so much time with older people like Lindsay and her family, I didn't think it was weird for a seventeen-year-old to hang out with another family. Sure, having a little kid around when people are smoking pot was a little strange, but, again, I really didn't give it too much thought. I was just a typical self-absorbed teen, and I mostly thought only about how I was going to have fun.

That Halloween, Nancy invited us to a party at her house, which was full of hot guys and drugs. Of course, there was weed, which was everywhere and no big deal, but there was also coke, crank, and who knows what else. And I, being a fan of the crank, well, line me up. My sister was at this party, too, so I had to be careful and not let her know what I was up to. My sister and I were still not very close. So we druggies went into the back room to line up. There was this total stud muffin there, wearing white, 501 jeans. He was so fine; I had to meet him. Soon enough, he introduced himself to me. His name was Jim, and, before the party was over, we had ex-changed numbers and had decided to go on a date.

It was a double date with Annie and a guy named Ryan, one of Jim's friends, whom she had also met at Nancy's party. Jim looked so hot in his white, 501 jeans. We got to making out in the back seat of my "roach mobile"—that's what we called my Datsun 310GX, the black and silver car. And it was hot and heavy. See, then I was seventeen years old and, yes, still a virgin. Virgins were hard to come by at my age. Most of my friends had been de-virginized by the time they were fifteen, sixteen for a few, but not many. Meanwhile, I still had that whole church thing in the back of my head, saying that once you had sex, you were completely ruined. Not to mention, I should know better, being Christian and all, that bad things would happen to me. I could get pregnant or catch a disease or just be struck down by God above. Who knew? I really didn't want to find out. I had always thought that I'd probably have to be raped in order to just get that whole vir-gin thing off the table. Not that I wished for anything like that, I just didn't know how else it could happen.

So Jim and I are getting all hot and bothered when he decides to ask, "So how old are you, anyway?"

In between kisses, I said, "Seventeen."

He gaped at me. "Are you serious?"

Clearly, there was a problem, but I wasn't sure why. I had hooked up with an older guy before. But I answered, "Yeah, why?"

He never answered my question. He just got really quiet. There might have been a little peep, an "Oh my God!" under his breath.

That night ended abruptly, and right afterward he dropped me like a bad habit, which was pretty sensible for a twenty-five-year-old. At the time, it didn't feel too good, but he really did do the right thing. We ended up being partying friends since we all liked doing a lot of speed. So if we couldn't make out, we'd just party.

That actually worked better for me anyway, because then the pressure was not so bad being a virgin and all. Being a virgin was like having a disease. People would either say, "What? You haven't done it yet?" or, "Can I please be your first?" I like attention when it's on my terms, but not the kind of attention that comes from being different. I always wanted to fit in, and, somehow, I never felt like I did. That's why drugs seemed so right.

I had all these different parts of myself all scrambled. I had the churchgoing girl who wanted to be good, the high school girl who wanted to be smart, the working girl who wanted to get ahead, and then the party girl. And I pretty much kept each of them separate from the others. It was a bit like having multiple personalities but being aware of them all. Somehow, hanging out with the druggies or party animals, whatever you prefer to call them, gave me comfort. And to this day, I totally get it. They didn't judge me for who I was, and they totally accepted things as they were. They just might have had a skewed version of what was going on, being under the influence all the time. I felt like no one put any pressure on me for sex or for anything else. I didn't have to be anything to anyone, and that was such a relief.

Now it might sound like I'm promoting drugs; absolutely

not, that's not what I'm doing. I'm just giving you another perspective of why I and so many people might have chosen to use them. What we found out was that drugs are always fun at the beginning; that's why so many people do them. If they weren't, we wouldn't have the drug epidemic that we have today.

—

By November 1986, I was using pretty much every weekend. It all went downhill during the week of the Oakland–San Francisco Bay Bridge's fiftieth birthday. The week before was no different from any other week, except I didn't stop partying for the entire week. Somehow, I thought it would be a good idea to see how long I could go without sleep. The human body still needs to go through the sleep cycle, or hallucinations come into play. But I didn't care about that then. Even though I had been up all week, Saturday night was coming up, and all I could think about was that I needed to keep the party going.

So, on November 15, Annie and I decided to drive across the bay to get some more partyables. I should have known this would change things. The first sign was, *Oh, my God! Can you say traffic?* We had totally forgotten about the anniversary, and they were doing this fancy lighting up the bridge thing, so, instead of getting on the bridge, we took the last exit and headed by the port of Oakland so we could go around and get to the San Mateo Bridge instead. There are a lot of railroad tracks in the west part of Oakland, and, since I had been up for almost a full week, I didn't see the train coming. Don't get too worried, we just missed the train. But it was a close call.

Naturally, that didn't stop us. As anyone in AA or NA knows, most addicts are pretty determined individuals. And we fit into that category. So on to the San Mateo Bridge. All of a sudden, I saw my life flash before me, and this was it! I was going to *jail*. There was a police car behind me with lights flashing, and I was totally freaking out. "Annie, what do I do? There's a cop!"

As I was slowing down as if to pull over on the bridge, where there wasn't a place to pull over, Annie yelled, "What are you doing?"

"I'm getting pulled over," I replied with pure terror in my voice.

"No, you're not You're gonna get us in a wreck!"

"What do you mean? You don't see the lights behind me?

"No, there's nothing there. Relax." I think she was trying to calm me down by yelling.

I looked again, and I was amazed, but there was no cop behind me. I could have sworn I'd seen a cop car with lights on behind me. Phew, I guess I had some sort of guardian angel looking over me that night; I didn't crash or get arrested. We got off the bridge and found a liquor store to get some Pepsi and cigarettes and decided Annie should drive. She hadn't stayed up all week like I had. As I was walking to the store, I kept hearing someone call my name. Every few seconds, I'd turn my head and say, "Huh?" I thought things were a little strange because no one was there. I actually started to feel like one of the street people who are always talking to themselves. So I got our Pepsis and Marlboro Lights 100s, which last longer.

We finally arrived at the home of our drug dealers, Janet and James. It wasn't in the best part of town; I remember that there was a not so clean African American man waiting outside the door, and we all went in. The vibe was very different that night, not so much of a fun party atmosphere, but tweaky, like skid row. I walked into the front room, and it was dark, but not too dark to see a white woman giving head to the African American man who had come in the door with us. Crack was starting to make an appearance then, and girls were doing that sort of stuff so they could get free hits off the glass pipe.

I was feeling very uncomfortable now. I liked to party, but, in my mind, I made a distinction between partying and being a full-fledged drug addict. Smoking crack was as low as shooting drugs into your body. I just wanted to have fun. And this was not fun. It was pretty gross, and I didn't feel safe at all. We were there for just one reason, to get our drugs. We'd normally hang out for a while, but not this time. I wanted to get our stuff and get the heck out of there.

We got our stuff—and I might add it was some good shit—and left to go get high somewhere else. Some of it was pure crystal meth, not like the chicken crank that's clumpy and yellowish brown. Naturally we partied like rock stars and had to go to work the next morning. Since we were out of drugs, I thought I had better load up on some Vivarin and Coca-Cola—another not so bright idea.

The day started like any usual Sunday. I had sections one and two, which were big sections in the restaurant. But, all of a sudden, right in the middle of taking a customer's order, I didn't feel well. I left the customer sitting there and fled to the back of the store, where my boss took one look at me and said, "Oh my. Are you all right? You're shaking, and your color looks terrible. You're all yellow."

"Can I go upstairs for a few minutes?" I asked. By now, I was completely freaking out. Annie had to help me upstairs, and I thought I was going to die. I lay down on one of the couches, and I swear I could see myself shrinking. My wrists looked like they were getting smaller and smaller. My heart was pounding fast and hard, and my blood was pulsating throughout my whole body. *This is it*, I thought. *I'm actually gonna die in the Five and Dime.*

Mr. Erickson was the manager that day, thank God. He was one of our friends and occasionally partied with us. He only drank; he never did drugs. He and Annie flirted quite a bit and later became boyfriend and girlfriend. So he was more than a manager to me. He was a friend, and I knew I could trust him to cover for me. He said to Annie, "She needs to get out of here. She needs to call her mom."

I knew he meant well, but all I could think was, *Oh, hell, if he calls my mom, I don't know what I'll do.* I just wanted to go to Annie's house and sleep it off, but no. My mom was a force that you didn't want to reckon with, and I knew at that moment there was no way God would take me now. Suffering my mother's wrath was sure to be a fate much worse than death—so much so that I badly wanted to die. She was going to make my life a living hell. He did, in fact, call my mother.

Sure enough, along she came to ruin the day. She showed up and didn't ask too many questions in the store, because that would have been embarrassing to her. Instead, she waited until we were in the car to start yelling at me. "What have you been doing? Are you on drugs? Answer me!"

"Your tone is making things worse. Can you please calm down?" I pleaded, hoping she would understand that yelling at someone in a drug-induced panic attack only exacerbated things.

"Well, if it's getting worse, I'm taking you to the hospital." She said, and off we went to the dreaded emergency room.

The hospital was no picnic either. The doctor yelled at me and said I was on the verge of a heart attack. He also looked up my nose and told my mom that the insides of my nostrils looked like I had been snorting for a long time, and that a hole was starting to form. I told the doctor I had only done drugs for a couple of months. I don't know if he said all that to scare me straight or if it was real. Needless to say, I couldn't put any type of stimulant in my body. I couldn't even eat coffee ice cream without going into a bit of a panic attack. That was such an awful feeling.

The following Monday, I didn't go to school. The doctor insisted that I be put into rehab of some sort. So my mother and I went rehab shopping. We went to an inpatient unit with people on beds coming off whatever drug they'd been taking, and my mom freaked out. The people we saw had been doing drugs much longer than I, and it showed in their skin. What a rude awakening for my naïve mother. She was very disturbed by the people in rehab and didn't want me in a facility that would be what she deemed "low-life." Actually, I hadn't thought the place was that bad. I only remember going to the one place, and, apparently, that was enough for my mom. She was a bit of a prude and had never been exposed to such people. She thought it would be best if I did an outside program instead, so I had to begin going to Narcotics Anonymous.

I felt that I really didn't belong in NA, as I had just started doing drugs three months earlier. The people there had been doing them much longer and had some pretty hard lives. Not me. My life, I thought, was pretty tame compared to what all my friends had been through. I also rationalized my incident; if I drank too much one night, I puked my guts out, and if I stayed up too long and did too much crank, I over-amped. That was my justification at seventeen years old. Stimulus and response was pretty much my thought process. So I quit drugs for a few weeks. I didn't stop hanging out with the same people that I partied with, so eventually I started doing drugs again, though I never went for days without sleep. I felt like I had things somewhat under control. I didn't know how to have fun or feel comfortable without being under the influence of something.

I guess I was still searching for that something that made me feel loved and that I belonged somewhere. The church was right, though. According to the church, once you became aware of the Lord's wishes and standards of living, and you didn't follow the rules, things would get very bad. I hadn't fully quit going to church, but I was living a double life again. I would go to church sometimes, and I believed God was sure to punish me for being rebellious. Things got bad, and I overdosed on speed. I almost died, and that really gave me a head trip.

Guilt was beginning to consume my thoughts. The church wasn't the only source of guilt; Mother was good at that, too. She had a way of making me feel bad, like I could do nothing right. If doing drugs was the epitome of stupidity, then I was just plain stupid. First, I got sucked into a cult and now drugs. In her mind, I was the ultimate follower and incapable of making my own choices. But that accusation infuriated me. I had a brain, and others considered me pretty intelligent at times. I just thought I was a typical teenager, exploring the world and everything, good or bad, that it had to offer. So I just kept on exploring. . . .

Chapter 6

THE DEED AND DATING

I really was having a lot of fun partying, aside from the over-dose, and I loved hanging out with new guys. I was great at making out and doing other things as long as I wasn't doing "the deed," but I tended to be attracted to older guys, and they were interested in more than making out. I was so naïve at that time, in the sense that I trusted that my new partying friends were actually trustworthy and nice, until I got myself into a precarious situation. My friend Nancy was having a New Year's rager, and she always put on a great party. Obviously, I had to go. There would be really hot guys there.

Jim was at this party, as he had been at the Halloween party, and I wanted to make him jealous. It was easy to do because this very cute, intriguing guy named Scott was there. That name was intriguing in itself, since I had dated a pretty cute guy named Scott in the ninth grade (who had dumped me for not putting out). But I had my eyes on him. We started to flirt and dance. He could dance, or he thought he could. Then we decided to go into one of the bedrooms to make out. At least that's what I thought we were going to do. It was pretty hot and heavy, then things took a different turn from what I was used to.

He was trying to take my pants off, and I whispered, "Don't."

He assured me, "It'll be all right." He continued to kiss me, and he managed to get my pants off. I'd been half-naked with Sal and few other guys, but I was used to them not pushing too far, but then his pants were off as well.

"I don't think we should be doing this, especially here. I'm not even on birth control, and I've never done this before. Please stop!" I was getting nervous, because it felt like things were getting out of control. We were in Nancy's kid's room, too, and it felt so wrong to be in a child's room, disgracing his bed.

As he started to force me, he said, "You're a virgin? Come on, it'll be okay. I have a condom." He held both of my hands above my head with one of his hands. He was so strong that I couldn't break free. Then I began to cry. I thought, *How is this fun for him, while I'm crying? Shit! This is really happening. I don't even know this guy.* This guy was skinny and pretty scrawny, but, man, he was strong. I was scared at this point, but I didn't want to make a scene. And I was half-naked. I was pretty strong too, but not strong enough that night.

I had really mixed emotions about what had happened. I really hadn't expected it. I actually thought when you said no it *meant* no. That's how naïve I was, and I was used to the church boys. I had gone pretty far with Sal, but he never would have raped me—or so I thought.

On the one hand, I felt used, but not totally, and, as horrible as the experience was, it wasn't totally either. I'd had a premonition when I was younger that something like this would happen or I'd be a virgin for the rest of my life. I was probably in denial about what happened, but I wasn't about to think of myself as a victim. I forced this loser to pay attention to me. He lived at Nancy's house for a while, and I made sure to turn up there to visit. I soon became friends with his sister just to be close to him. I wasn't going away anytime soon. He wasn't going to get away with raping me and then disappearing; that would have been totally disrespectful. When I think back on it, I guess I had to prove to myself that I hadn't been used and that he must have liked me a little in order to sleep with me. I knew the church would consider me ruined for having premarital sex, but it was even worse if you weren't in a relationship.

He was a terrible boyfriend. He told me that I would be so hot if I lost ten pounds and got contacts. Unfortunately, other guys had told me the same thing. Looking back now, I'd been pretty skinny, but there's nothing worse telling a girl she's fat. It doesn't matter how skinny or pretty a girl is, if she doesn't believe it. She'll always believe the negative comments, and that's exactly what happened to me. I already had the disease to please and plenty of issues around rejection. He was also the kind of guy who would say he was going to call and didn't, or say we were going to do something and not turn up. He was a typical player. I seem to have attracted that type for most of my life. Something about the "thrill of the chase" or trying to please or to conquer the tough ones. The worst thing was that the church had taught me that when a person leaves the church after knowing God's word, very bad things would happen.

Because I was having so much fun in a worldly way, I had stopped going to church regularly. Not only was the church against alcohol and drugs, when I was using both, but I hated all the hypocrisy I had seen in the church, and I didn't want to be that way. So at nearly eighteen, I'd left the church for good, and then, *boom!* I overdosed on speed; a month later, I was raped. I was beginning to think that the church was right after all. I needed to be punished for this bad behavior. I deserved it, or at least that's what I thought. I was starting to feel guilty all the time. After all, I was ruined. I was no good to any man since I wasn't a virgin anymore, so now it didn't matter who I slept with or when, right?

After winter break ended, I told my school friend Phoenix about my whole New Years' experience, and she was very upset. "What the hell happened? And why on earth are you calling him your boyfriend? It's 'cause you're hangin' out with Annie. I knew she was trouble when I met her. Goddamn it, Leah! What's wrong with you?"

Wow. I really hadn't expected that reaction. I thought she'd be excited that I'd lost my virginity, but she couldn't believe that I would actually be with this guy. I didn't know why she was so upset. Even though he was a terrible boyfriend, I finally had a "real" boyfriend who was cute and a bad boy to boot. I finally knew what all my friends were talking about when it came to sex. And all my friends had boyfriends. Before, I had felt like a freak, because I was the *only* one of my age (except for church members) who was still a virgin. Nowadays, girls are proud of being virgins, but they weren't back then, and others made fun of me. I just wanted to fit in. Looking back, I can see Phoenix was right. I'd been naïve about so many things, but I was starting to learn how the real world worked.

The thing with Scott only lasted about three months. He became very distant, and I was upset about it but couldn't change it. The last time we hung out was on my eighteenth birthday. Scott's sister Jean, Nancy, and I went to a nightclub in Hayward called Frenchy's. I could get into most bars. Back then the laws were much more lenient, and the bouncers weren't too bright or they just didn't care. But this bouncer actually said, "Can I see your ID?"

"Um," I said as I scrambled through my purse. "Oh my God, I can't find my license! Oh great, now what am I supposed to do? I need that."

Some other guy who worked at the club leaned over to the bouncer and said, "Ask her the questions."

"So, um, where were you born?"

I know I had a dumb look on my face when I replied, "Hayward."

"Okay, you can go in."

I couldn't believe this guy and how easy it was. We had a blast dancing to all the top eighties songs. We were having so much fun when Scott showed up. He had been a jerk earlier, so I decided to make him jealous by dancing and flirting with someone else. This guy had been watching me since I'd arrived, so I thought I'd play a little game. I danced close him, looked him in the eye, and smiled. He danced my way and asked, "What's your name? Do you come here often?"

"No, this is my first time." I replied, checking to see if Scott was looking. And he was. That made me even smile even more.

"You want to dance?" The guy asked.

"Sure." We started dancing, and I could feel Scott staring

us down. He finally couldn't handle it and walked over to us and asked to cut in. I said, with a shit-eating grin, "No, we're dancing. Maybe next time." He was so annoyed that now he had to have me. There's nothing like a little game of cat and mouse. After the song was over, Scott cut in for the next dance. It had worked like a charm. I was pretty good at the art of seduction, I thought, and I pretty much seduced Scott. Or maybe he seduced me. However it went down, I ended up going home with him and having sex. I thought this would make him like me again and he'd treat me better. I really had fallen for this jerk. I guess I was living in fantasyland. That was the last time I spent any time with Scott. Occasionally, I'd hear from him, probably when he was fighting with his new girl. I was pretty sure he'd found someone else, or he might have had someone the whole time. I was bummed for sure, but I got over it pretty quickly. Next!

CARNIES

Easter break was in April, and that's when the carnival came to town, near the Oakland Coliseum. I loved the carnival. It was such a cool vibe with all the lights, the rides, and the cheesy prizes. I loved all that stuff. This particular carnival was in a predominantly low-income, African American area. Though other people knew it as "the hood," I felt comfortable because I'd grown up there. There weren't too many white people at this carnival, but most of the carnies were white guys. We knew that would be advantageous for us. Annie and I could get on the rides for free and stay on forever. The carnies looked like they were having so much fun, like it was one big party. Of course, I was naïve because I didn't realize that the whole carnival scene *was* one big party. These guys were young, so the hardcore partying didn't show in their skin or on their faces yet. Some of them were pretty cute.

Oh, my God! Annie and I went over to the Scrambler, and there stood the man of my dreams. He was gorgeous. Yes, I know carnies don't usually get a reaction like that, but hot damn! We flirted, of course, but Annie liked him, too. I was bummed about that, because she always got the guys. She was a size zero and I wasn't; I was more like a size five. Most of my friends were extremely pretty and I wasn't. I wasn't dog meat, just not one of the really beautiful people. Needless to say, I was jealous of Annie.

Well, a couple of days later, when I was working at the Five and Dime, Mr. Totally Fine walked in with his mother and sat in my section. Yikes! I used to get super-intimidated when a really hot guy was around. I felt like I couldn't walk right or I might say something stupid. I tried to play it cool with a smile and asked, "How are you today? Can I get you some water or coffee?" I was hoping he'd remember me and hoping I didn't sound like an idiot. I got their drinks and asked, "Are you ready to order?"

Mr. Hotness smiled and said in a flirty way, "Hey, didn't I meet you at the carnival the other night?"

I was blushing and trying to not choke. "Oh yeah, I remember you. How are you? Thanks for letting us stay on the rides. We had a lot of fun that night." By the end of his meal, He got my seven digits, and it turned out he lived in Oakland, too. I was on such a high. I knew he would call me.

His name was Steve, and we started to date. He was working at the carnival, so wherever it traveled, he'd go. So, naturally, Annie and I went, too. Annie had met a cute guy named Tim at the carnival. The carnies, as their reputation proclaims, liked to party a lot. Not like the way Annie and I partied. I was getting ready to go on the Zipper, when Tim started to panic because he had just slammed a quarter of speed into his arm. I didn't really know anyone who used needle drugs except for the pastor's oldest son (go figure). The crowd that I had chosen to hang out with was so different from the one I used to spend time with. Sure, the new friends were a bit wild and not exactly what most people would call successful, and some were real druggies. But what I loved about them was that they never once made me feel bad about myself. In fact, they were the least judgmental people I had ever encountered.

Tim was so high that he was afraid the big boss would find out and he'd lose his amazing job. A lot of the carnies were on drugs, but they had an understanding that they were supposed to hide their habits. It sounded almost like church to me. But, that night, Tim couldn't keep himself under control; he was freaking out so badly that the other carnies began to notice, and it wasn't long before the big boss caught him and suspended him from work for some time. Apparently even carnival life had consequences when someone didn't follow the rules.

I had been seeing Steve for a while now, and my senior ball was coming up. I was going with a real man who was twenty-two and could buy alcohol. I had gotten to know him better by this time, and I was beginning to lose some interest.

I felt like I was doing all the driving and paying for things. He didn't seem to have much class. Plus, he got arrested just before my prom, although he managed to get out in time. But the real turnoff for me was the fake corsage he got me. I was mortified that it wasn't a real flower. And one of his eyes was all red from a popped blood vessel.

Apparently, he'd had some kind of seizure due to his use of cocaine, which made him hit his head or something. In my mind I was thinking, *Oh great, this is going to look so nice in the photos.* He was turning out to be such a dream, *not!* The red eye and fake corsage were the straw that broke the camel's back. At that point, his only saving grace was that he could buy booze for us to drink in the limo. The thrill was gone for me. Remember, I loved the thrill of the chase, but I really didn't know what to do with the catch. The more he pushed me, the more I pulled away. By the time my senior ball came, I was thoroughly disenchanted.

On ball night, Steve and I shared a limo with some of my high school friends. One of them was a really good friend of mine, a sweet guy named Chris. You guessed it. I had my eye on him, even though he was in a relationship. We were totally flirting in the limo. The prom ended, and it wasn't a great experience, probably because I was tweaking. In high school, my nickname was "Speedy Gonzales,"—nothing to be proud of. Steve and I went to a motel, which is what most of the kids did. Honestly, I wish I had gone to the ball with a friend instead of a boyfriend—especially, a boyfriend I was losing interest in. After that, I pretty much pulled all the way away from Steve. I felt bad, though, because I think I really hurt him.

I tried avoiding his calls, but he would show up at the Five and Dime parking lot. I was curt with Steve, but he didn't get the message. Our relationship was pretty much over after the senior ball, but I wasn't finished with the carnival. There were some cute guys still. Annie and I got special treatment, even at the Alameda County Fair, because a lot of the same guys who worked the little carnival circuit also worked the fairs. I always hoped Steve wouldn't be working when we went, and if he was . . . ugh. I really didn't want to see him because he'd gotten so desperate. His mom wanted to get the senior ball pictures, and I really didn't want to make any sort of effort. After all, Steve hadn't paid for anything. I was momma big bucks. Basically, I didn't return Steve's calls, and, when the carnival circuit ended for the year, he finally gave up on me. After that, I started dating all sorts of people, since I was technically ruined, by the church's standards. The carnies had been fun, but that season was over. So I moved on to sometimes new and sometimes old territories.

Scott was still on the scene and still had me dangling. He really was into this other girl, which was probably a good thing; after all, things do happen for a reason. It's too bad we can't always see that at the time. But distractions are always a great way to move on, and there were so many distractions.

Annie and I went to San Francisco a lot just to hang out. Polk Street was a place that was safe for us. We were just a couple of goofy girls who wanted to have fun, and boy, did we! One time in particular was such fun that I still smile when I think of it. We decided to take a bag of Hershey Kisses and ask people in their cars or on the street if they'd like a kiss. Duh, like anyone is going to say no to a couple of young cute girls. It was an easy ego boost for the both of us. There were these cops in a car next to us and Annie yelled at them, "What's up, eh? Wanna kiss?" I was freaking out because the seat belts in my car were broken, and a new seat belt law had just taken effect. I didn't want to get a ticket. The cops just laughed, and Annie threw them some candy, so no big deal.

Later we wound up at the corner of Polk and Broadway, at a bar called Shanghai Kelly's. Somehow, Annie or I had gotten someone's attention there with the kisses. Now this wasn't just any night; there was some sort of rugby tournament going on. The Australians had won it and were celebrating there, and those Aussies really know how to party. We fit right in with those crazy characters. We were having so much fun, and I even met this guy who looked just like Ferris Bueller. He didn't like me calling him that, for some reason, but I kept irritating him anyway.

We decided to leave the bar for a bit, probably to check out the scene elsewhere, so we headed to the Pier. Annie was driving at this point because I'd had more to drink and was buzzed from my vodka Collins. We started flirting with this guy on the Pier and he asked us if we could give him a ride. He had some beer and said he'd give us some, so we gave him a ride. I think he wanted more than just a ride and we weren't feeling it, so we kicked him out of the car. Now, I had these mucky boots that I wore to the barn when I fed my horse, and they lived in the backseat of my car. This fool decided that he was going to take one of my boots. I grabbed it and said, with an attitude, "Give me back my boot."

He slapped me in the face and said, "Fuck you, bitch!"

Unfortunately, at that time, my natural reaction was to punch back when someone hit me. So I punched him in the face, yelling, "Fuck you, freak!" At the time, I was thinking, *What is he planning on doing with one stinky boot?*

Annie was yelling at me, "Get back in the car!" I was all fired up, so we drove around the city some more, and I guess Annie might have made an illegal turn or something. The next thing I knew, we were pulled over by the cops we had seen earlier.

One of the cops was telling Annie what she could or couldn't do, and being all buzzed and still upset from the freak, I got in the cop's face and said something like, "You can't tell her what to do," which of course, he could. I don't remember exactly what I said, but I do remember the cop slamming handcuffs on me and attaching them to the steering wheel of the paddy wagon. I had such skinny wrists that I slipped out of the cuffs.

The cop looked at me and said, "You are from Oakland, aren't you?" I was thinking, *What does getting out of handcuffs have to do with Oakland?* I finally realized he had run my license plate number. That's what booze does to you—it makes you stupid.

After that, we got to talking. "Hey, where are you guys going?" the cop asked.

"Shanghai Kelly's, they're having a party with a bunch of Aussies. I think they won some rugby championship," I replied.

"Sounds like fun. I think it's time to get off work." He glanced at his partner, then said, "You all want to follow us to the station to drop the van off? We'll go with you."

This could be interesting, I thought. The next thing I knew, we were following them to the police station so they could drop off their van and go party with us.

As we headed to the bar, the cop named Jim sat in the backseat with me, and for some reason I felt like he was intrigued by me. He asked me lots of questions, like what I did, if I was in school or working. He knew I was under twenty-one, since he got that information off my license. But we were in a bar, and he paid for all my drinks. So the rest of the night had some blurry parts, but I remember that we left the bar and went to Ghirardelli Square to make out. We exchanged phone numbers, and he actually called the next day. We ended up at the Cliff House and Ocean Beach, and that was the beginning of our dating.

Dating a cop was totally different than dating the hoodlums I was used to hanging out with. It's always good to try new things. It was like having special privileges. Cops could speed, go through red lights, scare people when someone tried to hit on their girlfriends, and go to bars. When we were leaving the Cliff House, these guys made some rude, ogling comments to me. I'm not sure exactly what Jim said, because he told me to keep going, but these guys yelled an apology to me, and they looked like they'd had the fear of God put into them. I remembered seeing Jim open his jacket, and I'm sure they saw that he had a gun.

Jim was a true gentleman. He treated me with respect and was a genuinely nice guy. He called when he said he would and he took me to nice places. I felt safe with him around. Unfortunately, that all added up to a sense that things were going *too* smoothly and were *too* easy—which, unfortunately for me, was the kiss of death. I was into the chase, not the catch. I had caught him, and now what? It was boring, and I needed drama; that's what I was used to. And that's when I met Spider.

It was the summer of 1988. Guns and Roses was just becoming popular, and the midway was blasting "Sweet Child O' Mine." Spider ran a game, something like throwing softballs into a leaning bucket. Most people couldn't win, because there was a coin in the bucket that would push the ball out again (tricks of the trade in Carnie Land). He was so smokin' hot that I couldn't even see straight. Of course, we flirted, and when he took a break, we hung out together. He told me he was nineteen years old and that he was from Florida. He was on the carnival circuit, working the Alameda County Fair. His younger sister had gotten pregnant, and his mother was upset and took the baby to raise as her own. It sounded like he had a lot of family drama and just needed to get away for a while. There were many stories like that in the carnival.

The fair was almost over, but, of course, Annie and I were there every night. One night, Annie, Spider, and I partied with a guy named Rat, who ran the octopus ride at the fair and did some speed, and then we headed out to God knows where. I had to go to the bathroom really badly, so we stopped off in Castro Valley on the strip to find a place. You'd think with the boulevard being a cruising strip, there'd be plenty of places to use the facilities. Not! Annie had her Chevy Nova, which kind of looked like a hot rod, one that might draw the attention of the cops, which in fact it did. I liked Bartles and Jaymes's wine coolers, and I happened to have an open one in the car. Yes, that was a big no-no. We all knew that was illegal, but we thought we were real badasses.

It wasn't long before the sheriff's lights were flashing on us, and we'd been pulled over. Mind you, we weren't doing anything wrong, except driving the wrong kind of car. In those days, there was police profiling in every way, not just race-related. The cops didn't like any guys with long hair, because they assumed they were some sort of stoner or drug addict. This wasn't the only time we'd been pulled over, and I knew there was a risk going to Castro Valley, but I really had to pee. We pulled over in the AM/PM Mini Mart gas station parking lot with the sheriff behind us. There were two sheriffs in the car. They accused Annie of not using a turn signal while changing lanes, which she had. Spider and I had heard it. Then they mentioned that she was speeding, and she wasn't. Then when the sheriff was shining his light in the car, he asked, "Whose bottle is that?"

"What bottle?" I said.

"The one on the backseat floor."

"Oh, that one . . . We found that on the ground and didn't want people leaving their trash, so we were cleaning up." Good thinking on my part, right? I got really smart and quick-thinking when I was on a fresh bag.

"Get out of the car," he said. Now we had a flashlight shining straight into our eyes, which were dilated because methamphetamine enlarges your pupils. I guess it was a slow night for the sheriffs, because they called in more sheriffs—as if they needed two sheriffs apiece for us. I asked the two officers watching me if I could go to the bathroom. After all, that's why we were there in the first place, and it wasn't getting any easier for me. After making me wait for some time, they let me go inside.

I guess because of the sheriffs being there, the gas station attendant told me that they didn't have a bathroom. Really? No bathroom? Looking back now, they just didn't want me using their facilities. There were six sheriffs interrogating us because our pupils were dilated, and I still hadn't gotten to use the bathroom. This really sucked.

I'm not the world's best liar, but the sheriffs kept asking us what drugs we were on and where we'd gotten them. Deny, deny, deny. That's what you're supposed to do in that situation, but Annie couldn't do it. She fessed up. That didn't look good for me or Spider. They gave Spider a sobriety test while counting on his fingers, "Repeat after me. One, two, three, three, two, one."

Spider must have been dyslexic or something, because he failed miserably on the finger counting, "Um, two, three, one. One, two, three?" Like I said, he was really cute.

I thought for sure we were going to jail. We were pretty scared by that time, so we actually gave up a name and mentioned Rat. Of course, we didn't know anyone's real name at the fair; I'm sure they were all aliases. And no one at the fair was going to give up any information on anyone. So we wished them luck finding someone named Rat.

After a good half hour of harassment, the sheriffs told us to leave Castro Valley and never come back or we would be arrested, and I needed to find another city to go to the bathroom. Wow, we got kicked out of Castro Valley and never even got a traffic ticket. I guess the sheriffs were bored that evening. You'll be happy to know that I eventually got to use the restroom, much to my relief.

Spider came home with me that night and spent the night

in my car. Then, when the fair ended, he stayed with my family and me for a little while. My father wasn't keen on the idea that he was staying in my room, but my mother pretty much made the rules, and she said it was okay, but only for a short time. Spider was looking into staying at the men's shelter in Hayward until he could figure out his next plan of action. It was at this time that we found out that he was only seventeen years old. First of all, I'd had a boyfriend a grade younger than me in junior high, but this guy was two years younger. I was nineteen, and he wasn't even of age. Back then, I had my own little rules of what was acceptable in a relationship; older guys were not a problem, but younger ones were not my thing. There was a little conflict in my mind. If you had to obey your man and your elders, I wasn't sure how that it worked if he was younger. After all, that was what the church promoted.

Well, this was quite problematic for Spider and me. My whole perspective of him changed, like a light switch flipping off. Not because he had lied, but because he was younger. That made me feel creepy. So my family and I sent him on his way back to Panama City, Florida, on a bus, no less. Have you been to a bus station lately? The one on Martin Luther King Jr. in downtown Oakland isn't very nice, but it worked. We wrote letters to one another for a while and talked on the phone, but you know the saying: "Absence makes the heart grow fonder." Yeah, for someone else. I was on the prowl again. I just couldn't stand being alone.

Chapter 7

THE DYSFUNCTION CONTINUES

Annie's brother was always in the picture, but only in the background. It wasn't until he started to work at the Five and Dime with us that we got to be really close. Nick was very reserved and quiet. I knew he had liked me, and I liked the attention, enough that we got together occasionally, but I wasn't that attracted to him, and he knew it. Nick was really sweet and nice as long as he was sober, but when he drank he became a real dick. He was a mean drunk, and he'd be really rude and call me names. That's probably why I wouldn't let him go all the way.

Even though I set some boundaries with Nick, I tended to be attracted to assholes. I didn't understand yet what it was like to be in a healthy relationship. I hadn't even seen a healthy relationship except on television, and we all know that isn't real. Plus, the guys we were supposed to look up to in the movies were kind of jerks. Like Danny Zuko from Grease, the "bad boy" who smoked, cut school, and wanted to have sex. Or Rocky Balboa, a guy who lived in a roach-infested apartment and could only make money by fighting. Those were the role models in my day. Nobody wanted a goody two-shoes. At least, no one I knew. Nick (except for when he was drunk or on crack) and Jim had treated me the way I should have been treated, but I wasn't ready for that.

We were all working at the Five and Dime together one Friday night right after I had rejected Nick again. I was so fickle with him. One moment I would really like him, then the next it just wasn't there for me. It probably hadn't been a good idea to schedule us all together. That night, Annie and I were waitressing and Nick was the cook. The busboy, Ron, was our manager's grandson, and Annie had an on again, off again relationship with him. This was on one of their off nights.

Unfortunately, Nick and Ron started doing crack and drinking, which exacerbated the mood. That night, I asked Nick where my order was, and, as I walked to my section, he yelled across the restaurant, "Come get your order, slut!"

I was appalled and immediately went to the kitchen to confront him, "Excuse me? What the hell was that for? You need to act like a professional. Don't pull this shit here." Then Ron started to give me grief, so I told him, "Just go do your job." They were so angry with me that night. They'd been really moody since crack came into the picture.

Later that night after work, Ron and Nick went to the hood to get some drugs, and these thug drug dealers held them up with an Uzi, took Nick's gold chain, and threatened to take their car. I think these thugs just were having fun messing with a couple of white boys who had no business being down in the ghetto. I couldn't believe how my friends were changing. How stupid could you be to go to a bad neighborhood in Oakland to get drugs? Not only did Ron and

Nick get held up and harassed, they went back later for more. At least I knew what parts of Oakland were safe and what parts to stay away from.

Even though I was still using meth, I hated crack. Too many of my friends were going down that road, and it just was not for me. Their personalities changed dramatically; they turned into fiends who only cared about drugs and their next hit. I preferred meth because it was all about the social part of drug use, having something that lasted more than just a few minutes, and really mostly about having cute boys around. Even Annie was starting to act different. She had started working at another restaurant where one of her co-workers introduced her to crack. I didn't like the change in her personality. I guess this was one of those times when drugs were fun at first, then fun with some problems, and finally just a problem.

I needed to move on from Annie, because we were in two different places in our lives at that time. I wanted to be around boys and she preferred to be around crack. I was starting to notice that I could get more male attention without her around and really liked that. Most of my friends were prettier than I was, but now it was my turn to shine. Men started to like me better, and even Nancy's husband was hitting on me. There was something about attracting another girl's man that made me feel really special. That's pretty sick, I know that now, but you have to remember that at the time, my self-esteem was in the toilet. I didn't trust my own judgment or taste in men, so I went by how they responded to me.

One time a guy named Chris, who hung out with my Oakland high school friends, started flirting with me when I was driving. He was okay, but I wasn't that interested until Phoenix had a fit and forbade me to go out with him. *Yeah right, someone is going to tell me who I can or can't date.* So, of course, I did go out with him. Oh, she was so mad. She had so many other guys. I don't know why I couldn't have him.

Chris was another speed freak, always checking the window, thinking someone was outside watching him. It made me really uncomfortable. I was starting to get paranoid myself and didn't know why. Unfortunately, he was a player, and I got played. After we hooked up, he didn't seem all that interested and stopped phoning, and I felt like I'd done something wrong. I still thought that a guy would want me more if I slept with him. It wasn't like he was a real prize, but when someone played me, I would get hooked, lined, and sunk. It made me want that person so much more. I treated it like a game that I had to win, but if I won, what was the prize? A paranoid drug addict? Next!

I was no longer a virgin and still not a slut, but I was having some fun. I still felt rejected a lot and not very good about my decision to be somewhat promiscuous. First, Scott with the whole date rape thing, then Steve the carnie, Spider the underage carnie, Chris just because of being rebellious, and Jim the cop. I can look back and see that this all didn't start out very well. After being with what I considered to be a few guys, compared with my friends, I went to my annual appointment at Planned Parenthood to get my birth control pills. No biggie, except a few days after my appointment I got a letter in the mail saying I had something bad, some technical word and something about precancerous cells. *Oh, my God! I have cancer? That can't be!*

I went back to Planned Parenthood for a follow-up appointment to do another pap smear with a biopsy which, by the way, hurt like nobody's business. When they got the results back validating the existence of pre-cancerous cells, they suggested that I find a doctor with a cryo machine. I had to tell my mother and disappoint her once again. She wasn't that bad, actually, but it was something that I didn't want to do. We didn't have the kind of open or carefree relationship that other mothers and daughters seemed to have. Ours was quite awkward and uncomfortable, for both of us.

I was so worldly in some ways, yet so naïve in other ways, like when it came to my body, because I hadn't had any real conversations with my mother about it. In fact, our relationship was somewhat strained. I believe there was a missed connection somewhere in our mother-daughter relationship.

—

Later in life I put two and two together, plus years of therapy and realized how my mother's parenting style had affected my life. My mother would have described me as a follower in my early life. Being that she was more of a leader, she hadn't really understood my personality. She didn't give me much credit for the choices I made. I ultimately made the decision to do whatever. Of course, I was afraid of losing my friends or not belonging if I didn't do what they asked. I was the perfect candidate for a church cult. I was one of those kids who cling to their mother, and she was definitely not the type of mother who wanted to be clung to. She was never very nurturing, unless I was sick or it was a holiday. Although, there were some other caring moments here and there, I got most of my nurturing from the church and from my best childhood friend's family.

I was raised by a mother who was all for women's lib. Mother wanted Nicole and me to grow up as independent as possible, probably so we wouldn't feel trapped as so many women did in earlier days. Back in the sixties and early seventies, women usually went to college and then got married, or they went to work right after high school and then got married, or they skipped the schooling and working and got married just to get out of their house. Then, when women entered the "I am woman, hear me roar" era, things took a turn. They started to seize control of their lives, and the whole woman's revolution was in full swing.

My mother didn't take any crap from men and, in turn, wasn't always that nice to my father. It was at that time when divorce became popular. The divorce rate was extremely high in the seventies and eighties. Most of my friends had divorced parents, but my parents stayed together—although my sister and I were the only children I knew of who actively *wanted* our parents to get divorced. What my parents had didn't look like anything I would want. That's probably why I was never home. My father didn't command respect, which led me to view him as weak. Again, that was the complete opposite of the church, where women were expected to obey their husbands. Husbands were the strong ones, the rulers of the home. No one should demand anything, but you shouldn't let people treat you badly; not being a "mark" is a lesson I learned very early on.

With all the negativity in my household, it was no wonder that I had ventured out of the house to find peace. As a six-year-old child, I ended up in Oakland at a time when it was pretty rough, and I went there already having a great deal of fear. Going to church made me feel braver, and the people there were super social—albeit only among themselves and only as long as you followed their rules. Church also helped me learn about prayer and faith. It was and still is a great help in facing and overcoming my fears.

My mother was spiritual, but she hated church and the dogma associated with it. I think all my mom's talk about female empowerment, which directly contradicted the teachings of the church, was her way of not letting the church take over my life in the long run. Unfortunately, my mom taught me way too well that I didn't need anybody's money for anything. That was good and bad at the same time. I was super responsible with finances and in the workplace, but my attitude of "I don't need a man's money" led to my getting guys without jobs, as you will read about throughout this book.

Moms are supposed to be nurturing and loving. They are supposed to love you unconditionally. Just as the church had conditions and rules, so did my mom. My mother had obsessive compulsive disorder. There was a lot of joking around that in the family, and even she would joke about it. We had to load the dishwasher a certain way or it was no good. She wouldn't let us decorate the Christmas tree because we might not balance the color or size of the ornaments. Her senses were extremely heightened, especially her sense of smell. Perfume was a definite no-no. She was brilliant in everything she did, but she never completed some things, for fear that they wouldn't turn out perfect. Making decisions was quite a chore for her as a result. Most people know you can always do something over, but not in her mind—for her, perfection was the only acceptable outcome. I remember her getting a new job doing graphic design work, but she didn't make it past the probationary period because she kept telling her boss how things ought to be run.

It was frustrating to be on the receiving end of her beliefs. After watching lots of episodes of *The Big Bang Theory*, I'm convinced my mother probably had some form of Asperger's, or was at least on the spectrum. People didn't have all these diagnoses that we have today. You were just maybe not a people person, or you missed certain social cues. My mother had the same friends throughout her whole life, but kept it to just a close few. OCD is really hard on the person who has it. Their way of thinking is that the world should be a certain way, and when that doesn't happen, they experience all kinds of disappointment. As most of us know, the world does not adapt to you, but you must learn to adapt to this world. I know there were many times when I disappointed my mother or wasn't quite the daughter that she had in mind, or maybe she didn't have a specific plan, but I know that I let her down in some ways.

First of all, her pregnancy with me wasn't a very good experience for her. When I was born, she had some hemorrhoid problems which led to a painful surgery. As a result, she remained in the hospital while my dad and grandma took care of me for the first few days. Somehow, I felt like she blamed me, because she brought up more than once how terrible that pregnancy and delivery had been. If she hadn't been pregnant with me, she would never have had to experience the pain. I guess you could say I started out my adventure in this life as a pain in the ass. I don't really know for sure, but I don't think she bonded with me the way a mother would naturally bond. She told me sometime before we left Hayward not to kiss her on the mouth because of germs. Most moms don't care about germs, when dealing with their own child.

I went to one particular therapist who was traumatized when I told her that story. When you grow up in a dysfunctional environment, you don't have anything to judge by, so you really aren't aware of how screwed up you are until later, when it sneaks up on you in your own relationships.

Despite my hurt as a child, I consider myself the lucky one. I have and will continue to overcome my own issues, but my mother's personal hell would end up killing her at the end of 2009. Being constantly disappointed or let down will often cause you to be sick. That negativity stores itself in the body. I believe that is what caused my mother's cancer in 2005.

I was at work doing hair at the time, when one of her friends who was a client of mine asked, "Is something going on with your mother? She isn't returning phone calls or emails."

"Not that I know of," I said. That was odd because if she didn't want to talk to you, she'd just shoot you an email. She worked the graveyard shift, so that wasn't all that uncommon. I thought about it some more and replied, "You know, she did mention something about her ulcerative colitis acting up and being super tired. Maybe she went in to have a transfusion or something." She'd had that back when I was little. So I started digging. I called the house and even my dad wouldn't answer or call back if I left a message. What was going on? I really wasn't thinking of anything bad. I called my sister, then my aunt, then Grandma. There was something going on and I was determined to figure it out.

No one knew anything, or at least that was what they were supposed to say. I snooped so hard that day that finally my dad called me at work, no less, and announced, "Your mom just had surgery to remove twelve inches of her colon. Her spleen got nicked so they took that, too. Your mother has cancer, stage two and a half." I learned later that cancer doesn't come in half stages. I went to the hospital as soon as I was done with work. Boy, did I get it.

"How could you call my mother? You just had to go snooping around and not let things alone." She was so mad that I called Grandma.

"Really? You have cancer and you weren't letting us know? What if you'd died on the operating table? You're the one who's mad!?" I was just as mad that she didn't even tell us she was having major surgery, let alone *cancer*! No one had ever had cancer in my family. You heard the word *cancer* and think immediately it's a death sentence. As usual, she turned the conversation back on me.

"I'm the one with the issue. Yet you still need it to be all about you? I was going to tell everyone once I knew exactly what there was to tell. I wanted to know if it had spread and do research some on what my options were. Here," she said, handing me a paper with information about her cancer. "Read this."

The first thing that stood out on this paper was "one to five years if not treated." I thought, *I have only five years left with her.* Little did I know how true that would be. After reading it further, I found it really said that without treatment, 80 percent of people would not make it past five years.

I tried to ignite a relationship, "Well, maybe this is one of those things that will bring us all closer together."

I was trying to hold back tears when she snapped, "Give me a break!" with her finger down her throat, with a tube in it (mind you, she was in the hospital). She had made it clear to Nicole and me that she was not interested in being our friend. She was only interested in being our mom.

OCD comes with some narcissistic traits. When I say that, I don't mean the type of narcissism that demands your undivided attention. It was more about how things were in her personal world. Cancer had no room in her personal world. My mom was not happy about this cancer business, which is pretty normal, but her anger went to a whole new level. She was mad at the world, "How come this happened to me? I don't drink or smoke! I thought your father would go first; he eats junk, drinks, and smokes." I think she was mad at him for not having it because he ate mostly red meat, potatoes, hardly any vegetables or fruit, smoked tons, and drank alcohol every night to get pretty lit. Probably to drown out her negativity.

At that time, I believe my dad and I became my mom's punching bags. Nicole would never take that sort of abuse from anyone, not even Mother. I was scared, and how do you possibly comfort someone who knows that their days are numbered? My mother and I have had our differences, but we were close in some ways. She was still my mother, no matter what. Your mother is the first person in your life unless you have a twin.

She went through a lot of chemotherapy, but it wasn't successful. She had two types of cancer cells in her body and, of course, they weren't like other cancer cells; they were rare. One of the types didn't have a blood supply to the cells, so chemo was ineffective, as chemo needs to travel through the bloodstream to get to the cancer cells.

She had many surgeries to cut out the cancerous parts. There came a point where they couldn't take any more out. She had lost her spleen, a lot of her colon and intestines, her stomach wall lining, which was replaced a couple of times, her appendix, and possibly something I'm forgetting. As a last resort, she went to Baltimore for a crazy experimental treatment called a lavage, where they put chemo directly onto the cancerous area by cutting you open. Apparently, it's extremely dangerous, but she handled the surgery like a champ. Her cancer was never declared in remission.

A few months before the five-year mark was when everything started to go downhill with my mom's cancer. It was the beginning of November 2009, when I was about to give notice at the salon where I had been working, and my mother came over to my house for a haircut. She sat on my couch and said to me, with fear in her voice and her eyes watering, "I can feel my body changing and not for the good."

I asked, with tears forming but trying to be strong, "What do you mean?" I always hated when my mom cried. She was so stoic and strong that if she cried that meant something really bad was going on with her.

She replied, "Things are moving, and I think the cancer is growing into places that it shouldn't be." Now she was full-on crying and sounding very scared. "I believe we are coming to an end." I wasn't sure how to respond. Mother was not the type of person to share feelings with her children. I knew how scared and sad she was. You could hear it in her voice. How do you comfort your mother in a situation like that one? Words can't really describe how awful that time was.

Mother was very upset that her time had come sooner than she expected. I even thought that she would have died on my birthday for one last slam, but that wasn't the case. When my mom was pissed, she had some serious energy. I guess it was too much for her to bear, when hospice brought the oxygen tank and hospital bed to the house. Two of the transformers on the street blew that day, so there was no power. I know that was her doing. I'm so glad that I had to work that day, because that house had always scared me, and it was very dark up there on the hill.

Even on her deathbed, my mom wanted to control things. And because she couldn't control her situation, she was extra mean. We had her bedroom set up with all the hospice stuff, and I noticed she some of the family pictures on her dresser. I noticed mine wasn't there. "Hey, you don't have a picture of me? Here, I'll get one." I got my graduation picture and put it in the room.

"What's that picture doing in here?"

I was a bit shocked at her reaction, "I brought it in because you don't have one of me in here. And you have everyone else."

"Well, take it out. There's no room for it. It's in the way."

My sister heard this and said, "That was pretty mean and rude."

"It's not personal. There's no room for it."

The only thing running through my mind was *Wow, she's gonna die any day and she is still messed up. And you shouldn't bite the hand that feeds.* I was pretty crushed. It wasn't like she had to do anything.

My sister, my aunt, the caregivers, and I were the ones doing everything. If someone had told me what I was in for with this whole caregiving thing, I don't think I could have handled it. My sister and I got a quick lesson on how to change a bed with someone in it. I never thought I'd ever see the day when my sister and I would have to change my mother's diaper. We fed her. We gave her medicine, pain killers, and anti-psychotic pills. Then, at one terrible point, my mother's body made its own colostomy; the cancer ate through her body and made an opening through her skin. Her body had gone septic and filled with toxic fluid which needed to come out somehow. Needless to say, I learned how to put a colostomy bag on and off. It was probably the most disgusting thing I had ever have to deal with, but when you're in the midst of it all, you manage to do it like it was second nature.

My mother lost her battle with cancer a couple weeks before her sixty-eighth birthday. She developed colon cancer in 2005 and died on December 27, 2009. I'm glad she didn't die on Christmas, but I knew she wouldn't have because that would have been too much of a cliché. She was a tough fighter in that sense. But I think the real battle was in her own head. She was the type to hold grudges and fixate on the

small stuff. She just had lots of disappointments in her life—
or at least in her mind. I believe that disappointment and anger had a huge influence on my mother's development of
cancer, along with some of the things I mentioned earlier.
This pretty much sums up my mother and why our relationship was always strained.

———

So, now, I had to tell my mother about my abnormal pap
smear so that I could find a doctor who did the cryo proce-
dure. We found a doctor at the Women's Health Clinic in
Berkeley, but it wasn't subsidized like Planned Parenthood.
Her name was Dr. Simpson, and, though she was great at
what she did, her bedside manner was a little blunt. After she
did the examination and read the paperwork from Planned
Parenthood, she explained that I did not have cancer, but
sexually-transmitted warts that can lead to cancer if un-
treated. Nowadays, they have the HPV vaccine, but not in the
eighties. So, all I knew was that I had an STD and needed to
have this cryo treatment that freezes the cells. I made the appointment and waited.

A few days later the doctor called to tell me that my
blood work had come up with something else. *Oh, goodie!* She
informed me that not only did I have condyloma (genital
warts), I also had gonorrhea, and I should probably also get
an AIDS test because my immune system was weak. All this
information came over the phone at work, mind you.

I was shocked, not to mention scared out of my mind,
and it seemed unbelievable. None of my friends had any

STDs, and they had been having sex for a much longer time and had lots more partners. Unfortunately for Annie, I made that clear to her. "How could I have a venereal disease and not you or Phoenix? That's not fair. You guys are the ones who've been around." Of course, I was sobbing at this point. I knew it was a messed-up thing for me to say, but I was so upset. It was one thing to have a curable STD, but a whole other thing to talk about AIDS. This was 1988 when AIDS was a real death sentence.

Anyway, I had the cryo appointment, and no one had prepared me for how long it would take or how much it would hurt. I also had a penicillin shot for the gonorrhea, and, thank the Lord above, I did not test positive for AIDS. I was cured of all these sexually transmitted diseases, and I was never having sex again! I went off birth control pills, so I would have to use condoms and couldn't catch anything else.

Now that sex seemed like nothing but trouble to me, it was so obvious that God had punished me for leaving the church. It is said that sex is an expression of love, but, up to this point, there was never any love involved.

I had better luck doing drugs and drinking, so that that's what I went back to. I was mostly into drinking and just used speed or cocaine when I got too drunk and didn't want the spins. I had started beauty school and needed to focus on that, too. Off to school, parties, and socializing I went.

I had started beauty school in September of 1987 after I graduated from high school. To get my cosmetology license, I needed to complete sixteen hundred hours of instruction, so I needed to clock in every day. It should have taken approximately nine months and three weeks to complete school with perfect attendance and going a full eight hours a day. I had to continue to work while I was in school, which meant it would be about a year before I would graduate.

At the beginning of beauty school, I had been partying quite a bit, and my mom knew it. She gave me an ultimatum. "If you are going to continue using drugs, you can't live here anymore. I can't have you doing this under my roof. You'll need to find somewhere to go."

"All right," I said. I was stubborn and could take of myself. After all, I had been doing it for a long time. I was responsible. I had a horse, a car, a job, and was paying for part of my school. *What was she doing for me anyway?* At the end of 1987, I rented a room from one of my partying friends at Beth's dad's house. I had met Beth at school when I was a senior and she was a sophomore. Her house was a party house when her dad wasn't at home. Her older sister and boyfriend had lived downstairs in the in-law unit, so their dad didn't mind leaving Beth alone. It made for a perfect place for me to live.

For some reason, there was a rumor going around school that I was some big drug dealer, and the school administration searched my locker. I thought that was absolutely hysterical. Me, a drug dealer? Aw, hell, I couldn't be a drug dealer. I'd end up doing all the profits. None of my friends would even let me hold on to the drugs we'd scored. I lived by the motto, "Go big or go home." I did a lot of partying, but I was by no means a dealer.

My stay in the party house only lasted about six months. I just couldn't handle it. My friend was a few years younger and still in high school. Her boyfriend at that time was a coke dealer, and it was always around. Cocaine was great when you drank too much. Unlike meth, you could still sleep. Between going to school, working, and taking care of my horse, the partying got too much. I couldn't believe the concept of "too much partying" was even in my thought process.

I had my wisdom teeth pulled in the spring of 1988, and, with all the partying at the house, I decided to go to my mom's to recuperate. My mom was always good at taking care of me if I was sick or something, and it was so peaceful and quiet there, compared to the party house. I knew that I couldn't go on the way I had been, so I asked if I could come back home. I needed to focus on school and lay off the partying.

Unfortunately, when I first started beauty school, I'd gotten really sick with something like strep throat, so I missed several weeks that I had to make up. Then I had my wisdom teeth pulled, which kept me out of class. Also, toward the end of my time there, the school changed hands, and I didn't like their new stupid rules. My mouth got me suspended a couple of times. Once again, I found there were consequences for my behavior.

Despite my trouble in beauty school, I still felt the need to be an achiever. I wanted to be the best at whatever I did, including hair. The school itself wasn't all that exciting. It didn't feel like a real salon, more like the owners used the students as slaves to make money. I was one of the busier stylists, which, in my mind, gave me value and self-worth, even if I was a slave. We needed to get all of our requirements in theory as well as practical, the hands-on stuff: so many perms, colors, pedicures, manicures, wet sets, and the like. If most students had to perform two hundred and fifty wet sets, I must have done five hundred by the time I graduated. I worked twice as hard by my own choice. I'd had a burning desire all my life to be the best at whatever I did. I loved a good competition. Beauty school not only taught me how to be a hairstylist; it also taught me how not to judge people. I'd had a preconceived notion about gay people, even though I had two aunts who were gay. I learned very quickly that what I'd been taught to believe about gays, drug addicts, and people outside the church was wrong.

There were a lot of good people who were nice and contributing to the world, like me. I hadn't hurt anyone. I had a very strong work ethic, was financially responsible, and was getting an education. Why had God punished me for doing drugs? Why had God punished me for having sex? Everyone else did these things. *So why me?* Was God so mad because, unlike the "worldly" people, I knew right from wrong? Did he hate me because I didn't treat my body like his temple? I had an internal dialogue running in my head, and I didn't know what to believe.

Chapter 8

YEAH, BUT WHO AM I?

After going through a lot of hard times, I was starting to wonder who I really was. Well, at this point I was a high school graduate, a beauty school student, a waitress, somewhat of a drug addict, probably an alcoholic, and still an overachiever. I was extremely independent, hard-working, and pretty intelligent. Even though I still thought I wasn't a beauty, I was still on my search for the perfect guy to "complete" me.

I graduated from beauty school and took my State Board test on January 13, 1989, which was a Friday. It was just my luck to have an important test scheduled on Friday the thirteenth. Not that I was a superstitious person, but when I had a test that could affect the rest of my life, I didn't want any negative vibes.

My sister was to be my model for the test. She and I still weren't very close, so I was a little apprehensive about asking her. I had to do my written test first, and I finished that in record time; needless to say, it left my sister and me with plenty of time to get into an argument. It was lunch time, so my sister decided to get some food at the nearest restaurant. "How long is this gonna take?" she wanted to know.

"As long as it takes. I don't know. Why?" I replied with probably too much attitude.

"I was hoping I could get outta here. I have things to do, too. Ya know."

"You knew what you were getting into. I told you." I started to panic.

"Don't give me attitude or I'll walk right outta here!"

I thought, *Oh, God, what will I do if she leaves me?* "You can't leave!" I pleaded with her. "Mom will be real mad."

Thank God the argument didn't last too long. I passed and got my license. This was a time for celebration. I couldn't wait to tell my friends and family the good news. Only later did I read my daily horoscope, which said, "You will be put to the test today, but you will pass with flying colors." I felt like I had really accomplished something big.

Now it was time to grow up and get a "real" job doing what I had gone to school for. Be a real grown-up. I had always loved the thought of leaving my parents and living on my own, not having any rules and being free. Although my parents weren't evil people and although no one fought outright or was mean to anyone else, I was never comfortable in my own home because there was such a lack of communication among my family members. My mother talked to her friends all the time on the phone, but I can't remember her ever just sitting down and talking to me. I know she did the best she could, but I didn't feel like I belonged there. And now I finally had an opportunity to live my life the way I wanted.

I was so excited because I got the first job that I applied

for. It was "the" salon to work at in Dublin, very pretty and classy. We served wine and provided great customer service. Even better, my friends Tim and Teddy from beauty school worked there. I started as an assistant, essentially doing "hair boot camp." I swept hair as soon as it hit the floor, washed towels, cut foil for highlights, neutralized perms, acted as the receptionist, and did other grunt work—but I still liked it.

As usual, I wanted to be the best, so naturally I was. I started getting asked to rinse the perms out more than the other assistants, because I was so thorough. I also knew how to talk to clients, unlike some of the other assistants, so I was kept quite busy.

I became great friends with Christie, another assistant. We loved the same music and the same type of guys, and she was just plain fun. She was always happy and kind of a ding-bat. She made me laugh. I wanted to introduce her to my new friends, because I knew they were her kind of people.

I had found some strays near the BART station in Hayward when Scott's sister Jean and I were hanging out there. Most of them were homeless teenagers or in their early twenties who had run away from bad situations at home. Jean and I had met these guys, Ryan and John. John (aka Peckerwood) was pretty cute, and Ryan had a distinctive low voice and was very tall. He had a good body, but I wasn't interested in him in that way. Instead, Ryan became like a brother to me. He introduced me to so many people. Being with him was always an adventure. We'd go to the Hayward Japanese Gardens late at night and party there or go to constructions sites that had beautiful views; anywhere we could chill and not get caught for partying.

Eventually, I took Christie to the B Street BART station to meet my new friends. That's where we'd meet up to find a cool party place. Sometime, we partied at the station. The cops didn't even seem to mind. One cop told me that he wished he was off work and could hang out with me. It was a weird place to party, but that's what we did. Boy, did I leave an impression on Christie that night. We were partying at the station when I heard someone yell, "Leah!" It was my high school friend Teddy. I ran up to him and gave him a big hug.

His girlfriend appeared out of nowhere just then and started yelling, "Fine, go be with that slut! I know you've been sleeping with her!"

That simply was not true. We'd made out here and there, but never had sex. So she started whining and crying, threatening to leave Teddy. I was trying to tell her, "I've never slept with him." She kept yelling, so I finally said to Teddy, "If she's gonna cry like a whiny baby, just let her go then."

I don't know how she got to me so fast, but she grabbed my hair. She was a lot taller, and there was no way that I was going down alone, so I punched her in the face. I figured if she hit me first, it was probably going to hurt a lot. I did what I had to do. Both Teddy and Ryan grabbed us, and Teddy's girlfriend and I gave the guys a pretty good beating, since they were in the middle. What a way to introduce my new friend to the group.

Unfortunately, I had already gotten a reputation for fighting at the salon. One summer night, Jean and I were hanging out at the San Leandro Marina and drinking, naturally, when we had a little altercation. Jean was the kind of person who needed tons of attention. She had been hooking up with a guy named Shane, but they were mostly just friends. He happened to be with us that night, and he was flirting with me. It made me feel special, plus it was pretty innocent.

Meanwhile, Jean was really getting her flirt on, but Shane wasn't giving her the time of day, and that was making her angry. I thought, *Oh, my God, she just needs everyone. How selfish.* Shane mumbled to me, "I'd like to take my tongue to your body." And that's when all hell broke loose.

Jean went ballistic over what Shane had said. "That's it, I'm outta here." I said, but she got in my way and grabbed me to keep me from leaving.

I pushed her off me, and one of the guys that was there got in between us, and that's when the fists started flying. We were brawling. It took three guys to pull me off her, but then she slapped me in the face when I was pinned. They let me go after that, but one of my contacts had come loose, and I had to take it out before I could go back to pummeling her. I felt one punch to my temple, and, normally, you don't feel anything until later, but it hurt, and I was super pissed. I body-slammed her to the ground and was just about to kick her in the head, when something stopped me. I thought, *What if I really hurt her? I could really do some damage.* My legs were super strong, and if I got someone on the ground, I knew what to do.

So I offered my hand and said, "This is stupid. Over a guy?"

She grabbed my hand and looked at me and said, "My brother ain't gonna be happy about this."

"I didn't do anything," I protested. "You started it 'cause

you couldn't handle the fact that someone was paying attention to me and not you." I still had feelings for Scott, but he
had a new girlfriend. He only called me when he was fighting
with her. I knew it was pathetic, but it was what it was.
Eventually, Jean and I apologized to each other and decided
we'd better go, because one of the guys had called the cops
since we were so out of control. I dropped her off and went
home.

The next day, I woke up with a black eye. Not a bad one,
but bad enough for people to notice—including my mom,
who wasn't very happy when I told her what had happened. I
covered it up with makeup as best as I could, but that's how I
got the name "Rambet" (female version of Rambo).

I really didn't like to fight. I think I was just so frustrated
that I didn't know what to do with all my pent-up anger and
anxiety. I hated any sort of confrontation, but if someone
tried to take me down, I sure as hell wasn't going down
alone, and I wasn't going to make it easy for anyone. Working with my horse kept me strong.

Jean and I started to fall apart after that incident. My
mom's reaction to her was really unusual. Jean and I stopped
at my house to pick up something, and my mom said,
"What's she doing here? Get that woman out of my house." I
had never heard my mom say anything like that ever. She was
so mad at me for still hanging out with Jean after our little
fight. I had never thought my mom really cared one way or
another, but I guess her mama bear instincts kicked in for
that moment. That was the last time I brought Jean home.

Christie was a much better person to be around, but Jean
could get good drugs and find all the cute boys. I didn't know

at the time if Christie was into drugs. One night, Jean and I had a party at her apartment. She was living with her boyfriend, Barry, but he wasn't home that night. Things got too wild and too loud, and the next thing we knew, Jean and Barry got an eviction notice. Barry was furious and told her she needed to clean out the apartment and leave. What he wasn't clear on was what she could take with her. She was very street savvy. They had bought furniture and a television together. She liked playing house, so she paid all the bills with Barry's money, and had all the receipts. We got the moving crew, some of her friends, Christie, and some meth to help her move. Barry worked the swing shift so he was not going to be around.

I don't remember how many of us were there, but we took everything. There was nothing left! Jean had burned the receipts and flushed the ashes down the toilet. There was no proof that he had owned anything, poor sap. He hadn't even paid for some of the pieces in full yet; he was so screwed. We hid all the furniture at some other tweaker's house.

I hadn't put myself in Barry's shoes to think about how this would affect him, or us, for that matter. I figured he'd be mad when he got home and found an empty apartment. After all, he didn't have any proof that he'd owned anything or that anything had been stolen. I had no idea how pissed off he would actually be.

A few days later I was at to Jean's house, and we heard someone yelling out front. Lo and behold, it was an infuriated Barry. There were many threats and lots of screaming. Jean was nonchalant about the whole thing, acting as if he was crazy and didn't know what he was talking about. That just made him madder. He finally left because he wasn't getting anywhere with her.

Shortly after that nice afternoon, we decided to go out to party at some park. We were cruising along in my car, when Barry appeared out of nowhere. The chase was on! I was pretty fearless and a good driver. Somehow, I was weaving between the oncoming traffic and the lane that I was supposed to be in. Maybe I was just super lucky. We pulled into one of Jean's friend's driveways, and the friend parked a car behind mine, so Barry wasn't able to find us.

It turns out when Jean went to collect "her" furniture that the tweaker no longer had it. He wouldn't answer the phone or the doorbell. Now, who got screwed? Karma is a bitch, and what goes around always comes around; always has and always will. Of course, when you're young, you don't have the knowhow to think ahead, but these things will catch up with you at some point. At that point in my life I hadn't given karma much thought. In fact, I hadn't give anything much thought—I was functioning strictly on the level of stimulus and response.

But then I started to feel guilty about what I had done with Jean. I didn't think of myself as a thief, but maybe I had been one after all. I'd been taught to play by the rules. I hadn't been raised to be a criminal. But for some reason I had it in my head that certain rules didn't count. For example, doing drugs wasn't hurting anyone except myself. Taking someone's furniture wasn't bad, if the person you were taking it from wasn't a nice guy. Gas stations made a ton of money, so sneaking some free gas once in a while didn't seem that bad either.

But these recent events made me start to think more about where my life was heading, since it certainly didn't seem to be going in a positive direction. I was on booze or drugs every day. I was stealing stuff and driving like a maniac. I hit someone's car at a party and took off, so I wouldn't have to pay for the damage. I was hanging with homeless people at the BART and getting into more fights.

This was not the life that I thought I'd be living. I was supposed to get my career going and grow up, not be caught up in all these shenanigans. I lived moment to moment without any thought, so I was still attracting the same drama; some of it was fun, but some not so much. I wasn't acting like a responsible adult. I was acting like a rebellious teen with criminal tendencies.

I knew I couldn't keep it up, so I started seeing less of Jean and more of my so-called normal friends from high school like Phoenix. They reserved their partying for the weekends and seemed to have their shit together. Some had jobs and others went to college. In my mind, I was ready to settle down and have a real boyfriend.

Scott wasn't cooperating, and Shane was paying attention to me. Even though I wasn't that attracted to him physically, there was something about him that I found appealing, a sort of mysteriousness. He had a son that he seemed to be a good father to. He was nice, not a whole lot of drama. So, why not? We started hanging out alone. He played hard to get, which I loved; I kept on chasing. I was the queen of the chase.

The thing that should have been a red flag, but that I didn't pay much attention to at the time, was that he never had the same job for long. He always seemed to be starting a new one. He was great at getting them, but not at keeping them. I was used to being the breadwinner with the other guys I had dated, so that wasn't a real big problem for me. He also lived in a place that was like a furnished motel, and one time he lived in a place that was a sort of halfway house for people released from prison. I really didn't know much about this guy. But wasn't that what dating was about—getting to know someone? I didn't really read too much into it; after all, I was living in the moment without a whole lot of thought. I was just happy that someone I sort of liked was sort of into me.

Chapter 9

A LIFE-CHANGING MOMENT

When Shane and I had been dating for a few months, things began to change even more in my world, because a lot of my friends were getting pregnant. The first was little Lupe from work. She, of all people, was a shock. We used to party so much that I could not imagine her being a mother. Of course, Annie and I teased her, because that's what good friends do. Then, out of nowhere, Annie got pregnant, too. That was a huge shock, because she was just a little bit younger than I. All of us made jokes about her as well. Let me just warn you, do not make fun of someone you know for being pregnant, if you don't want to become pregnant.

You guessed it. Even though Shane and I weren't really committed to each other at that early stage of our relationship, I end up pregnant. I knew it the moment I conceived. We were partying with brandy, and things were about to get hot and heavy, so we went to the nearest store to get some condoms, and there weren't any. The store was completely out of condoms. Not thinking too clearly because we were drunk, we decided to go back to his apartment and get busy anyway. I knew something was different instantaneously.

I tried to block it out of my mind. As the days went by, I wasn't feeling all that well, and I had asked one of my co-workers in the salon what it was like to feel pregnant. My cycle wasn't really normal, so I didn't know if I was late or not. I prayed every day that I wasn't. I wore white pants and prayed for my period to come. All that ever happened was that I got some messed-up white pants from a little blood. I thought, *This a good thing, my period is finally here.* Not a chance in Hell, I was just spotting. My breasts got so tender that my clothes hurt them. One of the girls at work kept looking at me as if she knew that I was pregnant, and I knew she was right.

I finally got the courage to go to Annie's house; she was still living with her mom at the time. I bought a pregnancy test, First Response. I'll never forget that moment. I peed on the stick and waited for what seemed like an eternity, but was really only five minutes, and then I got the results. I fell to my knees when I saw the positive sign. I cried and cried. *This can't be happening!* I was so devastated. What was my mom going to think of me now? I had disappointed her so much already. I had no idea how I was going to tell her. Annie and her mom just hugged me. They kept telling me, "It's going to be okay. Really, this is going to be okay." I couldn't do anything but cry.

This was worse than overdosing. No one in my family had ever had a child out of wedlock. Abortion seemed out of the question for me, not because of any moral beliefs—I was totally pro-choice—but because I believed that everything happens for a reason, so I thought there must be a reason for this. I also figured this was karma for all the bad stuff I had done. Finally, I knew that if I was given any challenge, I could handle it. I had always succeeded in anything that I'd put my mind to, so I knew that I could take care of a child on my own. Granted, I didn't really have a clue then about how much it cost to raise a child, but I thought I was financially responsible enough.

Knowing that I had to talk all this through with Shane, I left Annie's house and went to find him. We went to Chabot Park and were sitting on the swings when I said, "We have to talk."

He said, "Okay, what's up?"

"There's no easy way to say this," I blurted out, "I'm pregnant."

"How can this be possible? We're just friends. I don't want another kid."

"Do I really need to explain how this happened? Friends? Thanks a lot. Is that all I am to you? Friends don't get friends pregnant!" I was in tears.

"Just get an abortion. I can't be a dad again." He was really upset, but I didn't care about his feelings right then.

"You should have thought about that when we had unprotected sex. It was your choice then. Now, it's mine, and I'm having this baby with or without you. You don't have to be involved; I can do it on my own."

I had never felt so alone in my life. I still hadn't told my mother, and I was dreading it. Since I had found out I was pregnant at Annie's house, it wasn't a secret at work. We began to talk about it more freely, especially since there were so many people around us having babies. I knew it was time to tell my mother, because if she heard it through the grapevine, it would only make things worse for me.

My mom and I hadn't crossed paths much, due to my working two jobs and her schedule, but I had to find a way to tell her about my situation. Because it seemed like there wasn't going to be any good time to tell her in person, I decided to call her from the Five and Dime.

I began, "Mom, I have to tell you something. There's no easy way to say this, and I didn't want you to hear this from someone else, so . . . I'm pregnant."

She yelled, "How could you do this to me? You need to get an abortion. Why are you telling me over the phone? I'm not taking care of another baby!"

I knew she was going to be upset wherever I had told her, but her response was worse than I had expected.

"Mother, I've made my decision and I'm having a baby with or without your help," I replied shakily. There was dead silence, then a click as she hung up on me. I was thinking, *I didn't do this to you. I didn't even have you on my mind when all this was going down. I'm not expecting you to take care of anything. It's not like you've done a whole lot for me anyway.* I knew from the start that I would be on my own for this journey. I really had no idea what I was in for.

I only knew that I felt awful, with morning sickness and all, except for me it started around four in the afternoon. I really only had a few good hours in the day where I didn't feel sick.

On top of that, my mind was spinning out of control. One morning at the salon, my boss took me in his office and told me I wasn't working as hard as I should be. I thought, *What is he talking about?* I worked harder than anyone, and I had no idea where this was coming from or why were we even having this discussion. I realized that he might have brought this up as a way to control me. My friend Christie and another assistant had recently quit, so I think that's why he took me in the back office, to make me think that I was not ready to be on the floor as a hairstylist, that I needed more time. As if a year of beauty school and six months of grunt work weren't enough. I think he wanted to keep me as an assistant for as long as possible, since I was so good at it.

But I wasn't having any of his bullshit. There I was, already full of hormones, and I just snapped. I started crying and stormed out of his office and toward the front door of the salon. Before I left, one of the stylists asked me, "What's wrong?"

I said, "He thinks I'm not working? I'll show him what not working is. I'm outta here!"

When I told Christie what had happened, she replied, "That's why I quit, too. There weren't any stations available, and I'd been assisting for nine months. I just wanted to do hair." She confirmed that I wasn't crazy and that I really was doing a good job, because I took great pride in my work, regardless of what it was. She was one of the few who knew I was pregnant.

It wasn't long before everyone else in the salon knew, too. Rumors spread like wildfire in that environment. So if the stylists didn't know then, they found out really quickly. Once one person knows, it's only a matter of time before everyone knew, and there was one stylist I had confided in. I didn't care who knew. I would show eventually. It's not like you could hide a pregnancy. I believe most of the stylists understood why I quit. I simply could not make a decent living on minimum wage and no insurance.

I was so angry and hurt. I was really doing my best and working hard as an assistant. I thought I was close to getting promoted to stylist until Christie explained things. I knew I couldn't make real money as an assistant. It only paid minimum wage, and I needed to support a child. I didn't even have medical insurance. I'd filled out the forms for getting insurance through work, but I'd been a little too honest about my little visit to the hospital for drugs and was denied coverage.

Now I had no job, no insurance, and no support. My life had finally hit rock bottom. I thought for sure God was punishing me for leaving the church. Lord knows all the turmoil I had gone through up to this point—and I was only twenty years old. I don't ever think that I had ever felt so alone before in my life.

I remember being sick in the bathroom, puking, and my mother banging on the door and yelling, "Did you find a place to live? Because you can't stay here!" I just wanted to be left alone while I felt so sick. It was bad enough throwing up, but my mom wanted to rub salt in the wound. I remember thinking that I would never do that to my child.

As bad as I felt, I knew I had to pull myself together and find a job. Even though I hadn't been going to church, I still checked in with Lindsay sometimes. After all, she was like a mom to me, and resourceful—she had great ideas about how to find things or get things done—so I wanted to tell her that I was pregnant. I was scared to tell her because I really didn't want to disappoint her, too. Yet, she was the only one at the time who was supportive. She didn't judge me or make me feel bad. She was ready for me to move into her home with her family, even though she was going through her own marriage issues. I was so thankful to have one person in my life who truly cared about me.

Meanwhile, I was still working at the Five and Dime, but I needed a hairdressing job. My friend Christie just had gotten a job at Great Expectations in the mall, so she set me up for an interview, and I was hired.

I was really nervous about letting anyone know that I was pregnant. I thought they would fire me before the probationary period, so I kept it under wraps. I made it through probation, but I finally had to tell our manager. I was almost crying, but she was great. She was trying to get pregnant, so she was very excited for me. Unfortunately, I still couldn't get insurance that would cover the pregnancy, since it was considered a preexisting condition, but at least I had a job.

I was actively looking for a place to live, but that seemed a lost cause. No one wanted to rent to me because I didn't have any credit history. I never bought anything with credit, only cash. I'd been taught that debt was a bad thing, and that I should never buy something I couldn't afford at the time of purchase. I did pay for my phone bill, but that didn't count. I had my own car insurance, but that didn't count either. What I needed was a cosigner, and my mom refused to do that. She didn't want to be responsible for me in any way. I was really stuck. I wanted my own place, but I was in total limbo and feeling trapped.

Even though Lindsay said that I could live with her—and I did stay there for a couple of weeks or so—I really couldn't for the long haul. She was at the beginning of the end of her marriage. The church really took marriage vows to the nth degree. People were not allowed to leave their spouses, unless one tried to kill the other. A wife leaving a husband was unspeakable. Wives were supposed to obey their husbands unconditionally. I actually think that the church condoned domestic violence, if it allowed men to keep their women in line. Anyway, Lindsay wanted to end her marriage, and she knew she would be kicked out of her home and excommunicated.

I hated all the church's rules and my family's rules. It seemed like you were set up for failure from the beginning. If you weren't perfect, you weren't accepted; if you didn't live by my rules, you weren't accepted; if you cut your hair, if you danced, if you don't get the best grades, if you weren't a superstar, if you wanted a divorce, if you got pregnant out of wedlock. All these rules—and I clearly couldn't follow them.

I felt like the biggest loser. I was getting kicked out of my mom's house, and my baby's father didn't want much to do with me or my baby. I couldn't even get an apartment. After the initial shock, I have to say that Shane did hang out with me some of the time, though he would occasionally do a disappearing act. All my friends were into being young with no room for a pregnant friend. And the few who were also pregnant were involved in their own relationships and building their families. I couldn't hang out with them, and I obviously couldn't go to parties. I guess I could have, but what fun is a party if you can't drink or do drugs? Besides, I knew I had to start to think differently. I had a child to raise. It was time to move on from my rebellious teenage phase once and for all. And I really needed my own home.

Mom finally came to the realization that the only way

that I could get into an apartment was if she cosigned for me, so she eventually did. She knew that I had filled out many applications, but, without a credit history, I was always turned down. She must have really wanted me out. At last, I had my own place, though it was far from ideal. First of all, it was not in the best neighborhood. Although nothing seemed as bad as Oakland at the time, 165th in San Leandro wasn't that much different. There were drive-by shootings one block over on 164th. There were allegedly drug deals and gang activity in the neighborhood, and hookers hung out on the cross street, which was East 14th. But it was my new home, and I was going to make the best of it. The apartment smelled like stale cigarettes and it had fleas. But I cleaned the place like crazy, and I was excited. Even though it had all these negative qualities, it was mine.

But, in the midst of all this exhilarating, newfound freedom, I was also six and a half months pregnant. My twenty-first birthday was coming up, and I was to be legal and all, except I couldn't celebrate like a normal twenty-one-year-old. In fact, no one did anything for my birthday. Shane and I were sort of hanging out, and, somehow, I thought he was going to celebrate with me, but he went on one of his disappearing escapades. It was a day full of tears. I didn't hear from him for a couple of weeks. It was so weird. Whenever he'd come back around, it was if nothing ever happened, like no time had gone by. This happened throughout our relationship. He would disappear for days or months. I didn't understand his actions. I would try to bring up the fact that I didn't think it was cool to just disappear, but he'd make light of it, and I was so insecure that I would accept his excuses and try to work things out with him. After all, he had a son already and appeared to be a good father. And, at times, it seemed like he was really into me. At one point, Shane said, "I hope it's a girl." I needed to hear that. I needed someone to tell me it was okay to be pregnant and this wasn't a terrible thing. That statement gave me hope. I wished my mother were more understanding.

In the beginning of my pregnancy, I had to find a way to convince my mother that it wasn't so bad, so I said, "Mom, this is a good thing. It got me to stop drinking and partying. In fact, I'm going to AA meetings. Isn't this what you wanted, for me to stop using?"

"Oh, so *now* you admit you have a problem? I thought you were okay. I'm not raising another child. I'm done with that," she said in a sarcastic tone.

"Whatever. How come you can never see the positive things in life? Why does everything have to be so negative? You know they say that alcoholism and addiction are really a family problem."

"Well, that's great. Now you're blaming me? You never take responsibility for your actions, it's always someone else's fault."

Clearly, I wasn't going to win that argument, so I gave up. Besides, the AA meetings were just okay. I didn't have a really good story for why I was there, and I felt like I didn't fit in. The good thing that came out of going was that I met a woman who did counseling, which I knew I needed. I needed someone to help me make sense of my life and to understand this guy, Shane, with whom I was now having a child. I needed to talk to someone who didn't know me personally or have a bias.

My counselor was just okay. I don't think I learned much about myself, but I learned what addiction was all about and how it worked. I think I was too young to comprehend most of it, but she helped me to understand Shane a little bit. She told me one reason he might disappear was that he might be on a binge using or maybe had another girlfriend.

I didn't know what to think. I thought I would have heard through the grapevine if he had another girlfriend. And it didn't seem like he was on drugs. Honestly, we only drank when we were together, before I got pregnant. He might have smoked some pot, but I never saw him do drugs. I heard that he had smoked some crack with Scott, once, but I don't think that was a regular occurrence. Shane seemed like a pretty decent guy, except for the disappearing act.

Although my counselor only knew Shane from my point of view, she did her best to help me see without rose-colored glasses. She also helped me a little bit with dealing with my mother. I had to learn to communicate with her without playing the blame game. I needed to learn not to react so fast, because it would always turn the conversation into an emotionally heated fight. I had to give myself a time-out, like breathing for the count of ten. Breathing was the best advice. I needed to keep the focus on what I was feeling and take responsibility for my feelings, not give her power over my feelings or lash out in anger, which I was so used to.

My mother made me tell my family members about my delicate condition, because she wanted me to be the bearer of bad news to suffer the consequences. Lo and behold, by the time I had enough nerve to tell my grandma, she had already knitted two blankets. I believe my sister or my mom gave her the heads up. My grandma was so wonderful. She saw that babies are blessings, not burdens, and I was so thankful for that. My grandma is the matriarch of our family. I have always cared what she thought of me, and, frankly, she has never been judgmental. After telling Grandma, it felt like it was okay to be pregnant. I could talk to her about things. She even took me shopping to get staples for my new place.

I finally started to show by March 3, 1990, so the cat was definitely out of the bag to the whole extended family. That was the day of my Italian cousin's wedding, so there were a lot of family members there. In an Italian family, you might think that there are secrets, but, in reality, everyone knows everything, but they are supposed to act like they don't. I'm sure I was a big topic of conversation in the family, but, fortunately, the rest of them didn't act like my mother. Some were very excited at the prospect of a new baby, and my cousins threw me a wonderful shower in April at my grandma's house.

That was when I could finally bring up the fact that I was pregnant in front of my mom. The whole time up until then, I'd never mentioned being pregnant or had any conversations about it with her. It was a relief when she finally accepted that I was pregnant. She actually talked about getting a video camera for the baby. That was her way of finally accepting her future grandchild. She started to ask questions like, "Have you thought of any names?" I guess she finally figured out this wasn't going away. Maybe it was because the rest of my family was excited. Or maybe it was the fact that I wasn't living under her roof anymore. I don't know what it was, but I was happy that I could finally talk about it freely.

Annie threw me a surprise shower in May a few weeks after my family shower. Things were looking up. I could talk in front of my mom about being pregnant, and people seemed to be happy for me. Even Shane was coming around a smidge more. Shane and I had gone fishing on Bay Farm Island, now called Harbor Bay, and my feet got so sunburned and swollen that they looked like pig's feet. I was starting to feel pretty good about the whole thing except for feeling so large and sunburned. I thought, *Maybe this whole thing will work.*

Chapter 10

BABY IS HERE!

Thank God Annie had the shower when she did, because things changed around my thirty-fifth-week doctor's visit. I had it all planned out. I'd take a few weeks off before and six weeks after the baby arrived. I was so looking forward to having some time off. Well, babies have their own schedule, and it's not usually convenient. Although I finally had some sort of plan, anything could happen. At the time I didn't know for sure whether the baby was a boy or a girl, but I was convinced that I was having a boy. I had it in my mind according to my body shape, because I was shaped very differently from Annie, who'd just had a girl. I was all baby out in front. My doctor wasn't big into doing sonograms unless it was totally necessary, but at the appointment, she got a puzzled look on her face and said, as if she were thinking out loud, "Hmm, the heartbeat is very faint. It appears that it's not in the spot where it should be. We'd better do an ultrasound."

I panicked only a tiny bit, since the heartbeat was there, and my doctor didn't seem overly concerned, but I asked, "Is everything okay? Is there a problem with the baby?"

"We need to see where the baby is in the sonogram. I

think it might have turned," she replied as she was setting up the machine.

"So, the baby's okay, right?"

"I'm pretty sure; we just need to see what its position is. The baby was head down at thirty-three weeks, which is where it's supposed to be, and where they usually stay. So that's why we need to see where it is. There's a chance that it's breech."

"What's breech?" I asked. One more thing that I was naïve to.

"That's when the baby's head is at the top of your belly, and the feet or butt are coming out first."

As she was doing the ultrasound, she explained it in a way that wouldn't confuse me, which I appreciated. And that's when they discovered that my baby was, in fact, breech. "That's what I thought," she exclaimed.

"Can you tell if it's a boy or a girl?" I was super excited to see that there was a real baby in there.

"No, see, this is the back, and this is the back of the head. Sorry, it's going to have to be a surprise."

I was scheduled to have a C-section on May 17, but before they would do the C-section, they wanted to see if I could get the baby to turn on its own, by doing some exercises. When that didn't work, the doctors tried to get the baby to turn around by what is called a "version." They said it was a massage that would encourage the baby to turn.

It was definitely *not* like a massage. They pushed and prodded me so vigorously that there was a possibility that I could go into labor right then and there. Fortunately, I didn't, because I wasn't on maternity leave yet.

When I finally went on maternity leave, I loved not having to go to work, even though in the back of my mind, I was getting a bit nervous about the actual birthing experience and what it would be like to have a baby around. I was spending a lot of time hanging out with Annie and her new baby at the swimming pool at her apartment building, and Annie made it look so easy. It didn't seem all that different from everyday life, except there was this new, tiny person. It reminded me of when the church people had babies, and life went as usual. So, I intended to thoroughly enjoy my mini-vacation and get ready for this baby to come.

Little did I know that it had other plans. That might have been my fault. With everything that was going, I still had my horse to take care of. He was my first baby. When Lindsay left her husband, she met a new guy and moved onto a ranch with him. I didn't feel right keeping my horse at Brother Jackson's since I had stopped going to the church, so I decided to move him over to Lindsay's ranch. In lieu of rent, I had to clean stalls and move manure. One night, after shoveling manure at Lindsay's barn, I experienced what felt like the worst gas pains I'd ever had. They went away after a bit, so I didn't gave the matter much thought.

A few days later, I had to move all my hay—a ton and a half—from Brother Jackson's barn to Lindsay's barn. It was mixed with the hay of another girl that boarded her horse there, and I needed to separate mine from hers. Each bale of alfalfa weighed approximately 135 pounds, and I had to move a ton and half to one side of the loft. I guess that wasn't such a good idea when I was nine months pregnant, but I decided to do it anyway.

That morning started out nicely. Shane had stayed over for a couple of nights, and we were getting along well. It was his son's birthday, May 10, and it was the day to move my hay. I ate breakfast, and although I felt a little sick, I went to the barn bright and early. I moved all the hay to one side of the barn, and it was no big deal. Then I went to Annie's, and we went to the mall. We were in Long's when, all of a sudden, I doubled over with pain much like the pain that I had experienced while moving the horse manure, but even stronger. It took my breath away and stopped me in my tracks. Annie looked at me and said, "What just happened? Tell me when the next one happens, and I'll time it."

I got scared. It was only May 10, and I was scheduled for May 17. So instead of telling Annie when the next pain came, I'd skip one and then tell her, "I think it's just gas." It went on all day and kept getting worse. In the back of my mind, I started to think that the pains I had felt the other night might have been false labor. Annie had some of that. She thought she was in labor and went to the hospital, only to be sent home. My C-section wasn't until May 17, and I was not prepared to have the baby a week early. After all, they say generally the first child is always late, and I wanted some alone time, like a little vacation. I thought if I could put it out of my mind, maybe the pains would go away.

But when we got back to Annie's house, I still felt awful, so I decided to go home. As I was leaving, Annie said, "You call the doctor when you get home and call me if you need to, no matter what time it is!"

When I left her house, she knew something was going to happen, because I never went home early. It was very out of character of me not to stay, because I'd hang out with company for as long as I could. I went home, and, of course, I hoped that Shane would come over or at least call, but he didn't. I called the doctor when I got home and explained what was happening. "You are having contractions," they said, "and you need to time them. When the contractions are ten minutes apart for a few hours consistently, call us and get ready to go to the hospital. But don't worry: since your baby is breech, you won't have this baby fast. You have a lot of time. We'll get ahold of your doctor." I guess labor feels a lot like gas.

I swear I looked at the clock and they were five minutes apart, but I thought, *That can't be right. They're supposed to be ten minutes apart.* The pain wasn't anything that I couldn't handle, so I went to bed. I tried to sleep, but the pain was starting to get a bit worse. I would nod off, but I was pretty uncomfortable. About five o'clock in the morning of May 11, I couldn't take any more and I had to call Annie. "I knew it!" She exclaimed, then picked me up. I called my mother to tell her it was time, and we were all off to meet at Merritt Hospital in Oakland.

When we arrived at the hospital, I was scared to death! By now my contractions were a minute or two apart. I kept thinking, *This isn't supposed to happen yet.* I didn't know how to reach Shane. He had recently moved from his motel-like apartment, and I wasn't sure where he was living. Half the time he stayed at his grandma's house, and that's usually where I could reach him, but not this time. I didn't want to leave a message saying, "By the way, could you tell Shane that I'm having his baby," but I did leave a message asking him to call. I had Annie leave a message on my answering machine to contact her if anyone had questions about my condition. My mom showed up to the hospital with the video camera that she had just bought. She was going to practice using it that weekend.

May 11 was a Friday that year, and Mother's Day was in just a couple of days. Mom said, "You'd do anything for presents, wouldn't you? You could have at least waited until I learned how to use the camera." I'm always ruining her plans.

They took me in to get prepared for surgery. I was shaking like a puppy when you take it to the vet. Merritt must have been a teaching hospital, because someone said, "I've never checked for a breech baby before," and put her hands inside me. It felt like it was a free for all: *Come on in! It's a party!* Annie had warned me what it was like to have a C-section, since she had just gone through it in January. She talked about a catheter and all sorts of good things. For some reason, the nurse decided to put the catheter in before I had the saddle block. I had no idea that there was even a hole there. That was no joke! Not only was I having these contractions, but now a catheter? I mostly remembered thinking, *How on earth can a person go to ten centimeters to give birth, when I'm only at one centimeter and this hurts?* It wasn't horrific at that point, but a minute apart and pretty bad. I just couldn't see how going to ten would have worked out for me.

Once they gave me a saddle block, the pain of the contractions and the catheter went away instantaneously. It was a relief, but it numbed me so much that when I had to cough, I found the muscles used for coughing were paralyzed, and it was a little freaky. It was hard to take a deep breath as well.

Still, I knew the doctors knew what they were doing, and I really had the utmost faith in them. I felt some things like tugging and pulling, but that was it. My mom offered to go in with me since Shane wasn't there. She was the last person that I expected to offer. After all, she wasn't into blood and guts, and she had just barely gotten on board with the whole idea of becoming a grandmother.

In the middle of the doctors doing their thing, out came a gurgled scream. Then quiet. Then they pulled the baby out! "It's a girl!" Someone exclaimed.

"Really?" I was completely shocked. I'd thought for sure it was a boy, and my intuition was usually right. It was so easy for me to come up with boy names that I hadn't really thought of very many names for a girl.

"What's her name?" someone asked.

After a pause, I finally said, "Umm . . . umm . . . Brittany."

"Would you like to see your daughter?"

As they laid her on my chest, I had the most intense feeling that I had ever had. Pure instant love. She was the most precious thing in my life. I had no idea that you could ever have a feeling like that, ever! She was so amazing and had so much hair, and I mean a lot. She looked like Gizmo from the *Gremlins* film. She had huge eyes and was so alert. Unfortunately, that gurgled scream that we heard was her swallowing some fluid. The doctors had to get her lungs cleared before she could come back into the room, which was eight hours later. It gave me time to rest, a good thing, as I hadn't slept the night before.

Annie had been trying to get ahold of Shane, but he was MIA. I couldn't believe that a father would miss the birth of his own child, let alone not check on his pregnant girlfriend or whatever I was to him. In my mind I kept wondering, *Where is he? How will I explain to my baby why her father wasn't at her birth? What will the doctors and nurses think? Worse, what is my family going to say? What kind of person is Shane, really?* And the most terrifying thought of all was, *What kind of loser does this make me?*

While all this was buzzing in my head, as much as Shane's behavior irritated me, I had a new love: Brittany. She made me feel love in a much more powerful way. I was still a little hurt by Shane, as I thought even the most dysfunctional of dads would have shown up for the birth of his own child.

I stayed in the hospital for three nights and was released on the fourth day, which meant I spent my first Mother's Day in the hospital. I was so jealous of my family. They were at my grandma's house eating fettuccine, while I was stuck with hospital food. I was so bored in there that I was out roaming the halls, pushing Brittany all around the hospital. It was very good physical therapy and helped me heal quickly after the cesarean.

I guess I still looked very young, because one nurse told me that whatever I did in life, I should make sure to finish school. I told her that I had finished school and that I was working on my career. She asked how old I was, and I said, "Twenty-one." You'd think the nurses would have looked at my chart or something. She apologized. She thought that I was sixteen or seventeen. At my age, that was not a compliment. The nurse had such judgment in her tone, and I was sick of people judging me.

When I finally was discharged, I decided to stay at my

mother's house. We both thought it would be a good idea since that I'd just had surgery. My mother conveniently had amnesia and had forgotten how to change diapers and clean bottles. Fortunately, nursing wasn't a big deal in the early nineties. Lord knows I didn't need to give anyone any more excuses to judge me, so I decided not to nurse. My mother hadn't either, so I thought she'd have some insight on how to clean the bottles. But no—thank God once again for Annie who was the one who showed me. My mom wanted only to help with holding the baby. Honestly, I can't remember if she actually fed Brittany.

At that time, I still hadn't been able to reach Shane, and he didn't even know that he had had a daughter. A week after she was born, he finally decided to check on me and found out about Brittany through Annie. He came to my mom's house to see the baby, and it was very awkward. "How come you didn't call me on Friday? I thought you were coming over after Lil' Shane's birthday? You didn't think to check on me?"

"You weren't supposed to have the baby until the seventeenth."

In my mind, I was thinking *You idiot*, but I said, "Babies come when they want to, and usually not on their actual due dates. Any normal parent would have at least checked in." Needless to say, there wasn't that much of a conversation between us. I was hurt, furious, and embarrassed over this situation. How could I have I picked such a loser to have a baby with?

The next day or so I decided to go home. I was doing everything on my own anyway, so I thought I would be more comfortable in my own place, and I was right.

But the lack of sleep was killing me. You're never prepared for that sort of thing. I have always been a sleeper; I need a good seven to eight hours a night. But my little tiny precious baby was *hungry*.

Brittany came into this world as hungry as a horse. She had a hollow leg. Her first feeding was two ounces, without a blink. I personally don't think that I could have produced enough milk for that child, so thank God for formula. As a two-week-old baby, she drank five ounces of formula, and two hours later she drank six more ounces. She was eating me out of house and home. I wasn't making that much money, and formula was very expensive. I called the doctor in a panic. "She's eating everything, and I can't afford it. What should I do?"

Bless her doctor. He was the best. He suggested that I put a little bit of cereal in her bottle and that should fill her up. And it worked. She started sleeping through the night in an instant. She was such an easy baby. They say God never gives more than you can handle, and I started to believe that there was some truth to that theory.

Shane had come by a few times since I'd been home. One Thursday, when he was supposed to come over, I had everything clean and had prepared dinner. It was like playing house, but there was no Shane. After that, I didn't hear from or see him for five months. I tried not to let it upset me. After all, we hadn't started out in some great relationship, but I really wanted to try the family thing. I prayed every night that he would come back. I went looking for him once but had no luck. Then I dreamed that I had found him, and he'd thrown a Budweiser beer can at my head and said, "If I want to be with you, I know where you are. Now leave me alone!" I have never forgotten that dream. If someone really wants to be with you, they will. I never went looking for him again.

—

The monotony of the first year of life as a single mother was rough. Just the everyday things: working, grocery shopping, cleaning house, showering, taking care of the baby, and the occasional holiday or birthday party. There was a lot that needed to be done, and everything was so expensive, especially since I was on my own. I didn't get child support like my friends, though not for lack of trying. I called about child support, but they wanted information I didn't have. I didn't even have his signature on the birth certificate, because he hadn't been there. I needed to establish paternity, but how could I do that when he wasn't around? Not only did I not have financial support, I didn't have anyone to take her for a night or weekend.

I didn't have money or time to go out, even if my friends had wanted to hang out with me. Plus, they wanted to do what normal twenty-one-year-olds did. Annie babysat for me three days a week after I went back to work, but she had her own life. My work schedule was not a typical nine-to-five with weekends off; I worked Friday through Tuesday. But at least it was a set schedule. I had quit one salon and moved to another in order to get it. My mother had made it very clear that she was *not* raising my daughter, and I was determined that I was never going to ask her to babysit. I didn't either, and she finally had to ask me if she could babysit, about three months after Brittany was born. If someone tells me I can't do something, I'll do whatever it takes to prove them wrong. I wasn't about to ask my mother for anything. I didn't need her or anyone else.

Of course, that was a lie. Right after having a baby is considered to be one of the most vulnerable times in a woman's life, and she needs support from everyone around her. The two people who should have supported me the most were the baby's father and my own mother, but I had neither. Both of them were so wrapped up in their own drama that there was no room for me. I felt so empty except with this little tiny love of my life. She helped me more than I could have imagined. Although I was very busy with everyday life as a new mom, I still felt okay. I was sad over my mom's and Shane's lack of caring, but I wasn't depressed. I really did want the family and the white picket fence, but that was the only part that was missing.

I did a lot of praying during that time. I must warn you, though. Be careful what you wish for, because God does answer prayers. About five months after Shane's disappearance, I decided on a whim to call his grandmother, and he took the call. "Hi, how have you been?" I asked, and I'm sure my voice was shaky. I hadn't expected him to answer after all this time.

"I'm good. How's it going?" he said, as if no time had gone by and we had spoken the night before or something. It was strange, but I was so happy that he seemed normal and he was interested in Brittany and me. He finally started coming around quite regularly.

Around Brittany's first birthday he suggested, "I know things started out a bit rocky, but I've decided that I don't want to date anyone else and we should be exclusive. I really have strong feelings for you. I didn't want to have to be in this situation again. I've been married before and the breakup was too much to bear. I was hoping I'd never have to go through that again."

"Why didn't you tell me? I'm not like other girls. I'd never hurt you." I was so relieved to hear that he was a broken soul and, of course, I knew I could fix him. He wasn't a loser after all. He just had some problems. We started acting like a family. We went to touristy places like Half Moon Bay, San Francisco, and festivals. I loved every minute of it. I even met his sister who had a salon. I actually ended up working in her salon when I got fired over Brittany's birthday party. That was a long story, but not very interesting. I was just relieved to have somewhere else to go work. And why not keep it in the family? That's what it really felt like. I was getting to know his family, and he was getting to know mine. I was finally getting what I had been praying for: a chance to see if this family thing could work.

—

Shane was changing in negative ways, as well. He had a jealous streak that started to show, and I had never seen this side of him. At first, I took it as a compliment: *He must really like me. I must be really special; after all, I'm the mother of his child. We have this special bond.* Let me remind you that I still had never been in a real relationship before.

I was making pretty good money at that time working in Shane's sister's shop. I really wanted to move from my apartment, because we had new management who were not keeping the crack-head hookers out of the laundry room the way our other managers had. My apartment was right next to the laundry room, and I literally walked in on a woman smoking crack. I could smell it, and there were piles of matches all over the place. She said she was looking for her cat. Yeah, right! You weren't even allowed to have pets there. There were condoms on the ground outside. It was a lousy neighborhood, and I was afraid that if anything happened, there was a good chance that it would be in the laundry room, and we were right there.

I started looking for another place to live. The manager at every place that I looked at always had the same expression when they read on my application that there were two of us, my child and me. They would say things like, "You know there's a swimming pool, and there isn't a fence around it. Not very kid friendly, you know?" Or, "We like to keep things quiet; we don't have a lot of children here. There are probably better places for you and your kid." Not to mention, "Oh, you're single?" All the places that had those kinds of comments always came with a rejection letter that usually said, "We had a better applicant. Sorry." Again, I was being discriminated against as a young, single mother. No one would rent to me. They thought of me as a piece of shit, probably on welfare. Some places just didn't want kids in their building. I was used to racism, but this was judging my character. I knew that I was super-responsible. I always paid my bills on time. So, I asked Shane if we should move in together, and he agreed. I'll be darned that the first place that we looked at together—as a perfect, cute new family—accepted us.

The day we got the keys I, knew it was a huge mistake.

We had been in a fight when we were shopping at the Bayfair Mall. I said to Shane, "You don't like anything that I like!" Honestly, I don't even remember what it was about. Something stupid. And he began to pout.

We left the store and were walking to the parking lot, when Shane said, "What was that for? What do you mean when you said that I don't like anything that you like? What the hell does that mean?"

"Well, you don't." Lo and behold, he smacked my sunglasses off my face. I was a bit shocked, thinking, *What was that for?* I'm a lot of things, but not a chump, so I yelled, "What the fuck?" My blood was boiling! No way was I letting him get in the car with my daughter and me. I put her in her car seat which was in the back of the Toyota King Cab, so Shane couldn't get into the truck. And, when he tried to get in, I slammed the door. Unfortunately, his stupid hand was in the way. I was so mad! I locked his hand in the door. This meant that I had to unlock the door and let his hand out. I was in such a rage, that before I opened the door, I took the key and dragged it down his arm and cut him.

"You fuckin' bitch!" As one might expect, he was pissed. He forced his way into the truck and wouldn't get out. We got to my apartment, and he threw my keys somewhere. I never found them.

I had to get the manager involved, which was so embarrassing. How do you tell someone, "My boyfriend, the father of my child, just threw my keys out, because we got into a fight, and I now can't get into my house . . . can you let me in?" I did not like coming across as white trash. I didn't tell them the whole story, but I knew what really happened.

Here I was about to move in with this man, and it wasn't off to a great start. Not with all that drama already that gone down. I had no choice. No one would rent to me, and I couldn't stay where I was. So things had to get better, right?

Chapter 11

TRAPPED

The time came when we got our keys to move into a new little two-bedroom townhouse. It was cute and cozy, very clean, with a little back patio and the best part: a swimming pool. Finally, I would have some financial help. And I was making really good money working in Shane's sister's salon. Shane and I agreed to split the bills. I had already been paying for PG&E, cable, and the phone, so I kept everything in my name, so I wouldn't have to pay deposits. Shane apologized for being such an ass at the mall, and, like any other girl in an abusive relationship, I accepted it. After all, I didn't think that I was actually in an abusive relationship. That happened to other people, not me. He was so sincere that I honestly thought things might work out after all.

The move itself wasn't the best. I had my friends help us, and the part of me that thought Shane was sincere about his apology went right out the door. He was such an ass. He was so rude to my friends who helped us move. All the time they were working, he just sat on the couch. He wasn't even watching Brittany; she was staying with my cousin while we moved. He had the audacity to ask my friend, "Hey, while you're up can you get me a beer?"

With a look of disgust at him, and a what-the-hell look at

me, my friend rolled her eyes and said, "Sure, let me get that for you." Here, I got these people to help us move, and he treated them like hired hands.

I was mortified and immediately said, "I'll get it. In fact, can I get you something for all your help?" Then I went up to her and whispered, "I'm so sorry for his behavior. I think he's tired or something." I was totally making excuses.

She replied, "It's no biggie. Don't worry, but wow." As my friends were leaving, she made a point of saying, "If you need anything, I'm only a few blocks away." It was as if she was letting me know that she knew more than I had let on. I hadn't told anyone about the incident in the mall parking lot. I knew how stupid it would make me seem. Why on earth would anyone with half a brain move in with some crazy person who hits you? That had never happened before, so I really thought it was an isolated incident. And I had to get out of the crack-infested apartment building. Here, I had lot of red flags, but I chose to ignore them.

Not only did Shane embarrass me by being rude to my friends, but he was becoming more and more jealous. One night we had planned a date night. My aunt babysat for us, while we went to dinner and then to the movies. We went to a Mexican restaurant, and the waiter came up to us, as they do, and said, "Hi, I'll be your waiter. Can I get you some drinks to start with? How about you, miss?" He smiled.

"Just water for me, thank you." I said with a smile.

Shane's face started to change. He got this look when he wasn't happy. Somehow his eyes would get darker, and then he started interrogating me, "Do you think he's cute? Why did you look at him like that? You're such a bitch!"

"What in the hell are you talking about? I ordered water. And he will be back, and I need to order my food. Is that gonna be a problem for you, as well?" This was all so new to me that I was so confused. "Can't we just enjoy our night out? Why do you turn everything into a fight? I was just being polite."

"I saw how you looked at him. Do you know him?" Then he proceeded to give me the silent treatment and the waiter lots of dirty looks.

He's absolutely nuts, I thought. We still went to the movies, but he wouldn't sit with me. I knew I had to go home with this man and live with this. One side of me thought, *What the hell did I get myself into?* The other side of me thought, *Wow, I must be something special for him to get so mad when some guy pays me some attention.* Sometimes, Shane didn't want anything to do with me, and other times he was very possessive. I didn't know what to make of it.

The possessive stuff started getting old really fast. I thought it was good to a certain point, but then I couldn't seem to do anything right, which led to a lot of fighting. He would call my work to see if I was there. One time he called his sister's salon, and my friend the nail girl answered, "Thank you for calling, how may I help you? Oh, hi, Shane. You want to talk to Leah?" There was a pause, and then she hung up the phone. She came up to me and said, "I guess Shane is checking up on you. He wanted to know if you were here, but he didn't want to talk to you."

"I wonder where he thought I'd be." I said. *He's checking up on me? That's super weird.*

"Guess he thinks you have a little somethin' somethin' on the side." The nail girl said, chuckling. He had this crazy idea that I was cheating, as if I had time for that. I had never thought I'd have someone checking up on me. I didn't like it one bit. I began to realize that Shane was thinking of me more as a possession than a person. That's what happens in abusive relationships. I had never once thought of myself as an abused little woman; I had always considered myself strong, not the type of person to let someone treat me like shit.

As our fighting became more and more frequent, it also got physical. One day, we were having one of our everyday battles, when I tried to leave. Shane was standing in front of the door, and he pushed me. I fell and hit my head on our coffee table, and my head started to bleed. I called 911. "Can you please send someone over? My boyfriend won't let me leave. Can you please make him leave? I need help!" Shane was blocking the door so that I couldn't leave.

"You shouldn't have done that," Shane said in a very smug tone. "They're gonna take you, too. We'll both go to jail. I'll say you started it."

I panicked for a second. I didn't know if I'd get in trouble, too. Maybe the cops would believe him, even though it would be a lie. What if I had to go to jail? This was so not cool. But it was too late. I had already made the call, and the cops were probably on their way. The sheriffs came to the apartment and asked, "So what seems to be the problem? Did you hit her, sir?"

"No. I didn't mean for her to fall. I was just grabbing her, and she tripped and hit her head on the coffee table. We had a little argument, that's all." Shane was very cool about it.

"Can't you make him leave? I wanted to go, but it would be easier if he left, because I have the baby." I pleaded.

The officer looked at me, "Well, ma'am, whose name is on the lease?"

"Both of ours."

"In that case, we can't legally throw him out of his house."

Tears filled my eyes, "Why not? It's not safe for me."

Then the officer got snippy with me. "It's his house, too. And that's the law. You can leave if you want to, but he doesn't have to do anything." It was almost as if he was on Shane's side.

I called Annie to see if I could stay at her house for the night. I had to tell her everything that was going on, "Do you know how embarrassing that was? The neighbors were staring. And now they probably think I'm some abused girlfriend or something. And the cops said there was nothing I could do! I really don't know how much more I can take. I feel like the epitome of white trash right now." I was sobbing.

"Of course you can come over. And you're not white trash. Don't say that about yourself."

"I hate him! I just want him to leave. God! I really thought I wanted this to work, but I can't take it! This isn't normal."

I ended up staying only one night at Annie's, because Brittany needed to be in her own bed. Shane called Annie to see if I was there, and she told him that I was, but I didn't talk to him until I went home. When we got back, I said, "I can't take this, Shane. I don't know what you want from me. You're always accusing me of cheating, like when would I possibly have time?"

"How could you be working all that time? I know you don't always have clients."

"That's how you build a clientele. You have to wait around until someone comes in. And why would I cheat? You're enough. I don't even want to have sex! I really don't think this fighting is good for Brittany, and I really think you need to leave. It only makes sense, since everything in the apartment is mine."

"I'm not going anywhere! You're just gonna have to deal with it. It's my house, too."

"You don't even like me, or you wouldn't treat me this way. Why do you want to stay?"

"You don't get it. I love you, and no one will ever love you like I do."

It sure didn't feel like love to me, nor did I know what to call it. At twenty-two, I knew that life was too short to live that way. I had not been raised that way; there was no domestic violence in my home growing up. I may have been around it, but not in my own family; men didn't hit their women. I had to find a way to get out of this situation, but he wouldn't leave.

As if I didn't already hate my life, Shane decided he wasn't going to pay for anything. Our agreement when we moved into the apartment was to split all the bills in half. We had both signed the lease for the apartment, but everything else was in my name, which was a huge mistake on my part. I was dumbfounded when he said, so nonchalantly, "I'm not giving you any money."

"What? You said . . . Why don't you just leave, then? I'll give you the deposit you put down on this place, and you can go somewhere else. I have all my stuff here and Brittany. It would be easier if you just left." *Why should he leave? He has it made. I work really hard,* I thought. I knew I could make it on my own, since I was doing so well financially.

———

I was elated about the money I was finally making, $600–$700 a week. That was great, since at the other salon I'd only been making $500 every two weeks. Because the rent on our place was only $695 a month, I knew that if Shane and I actually split up, I could handle the rent on my own. I was probably a little too excited. One day, I was getting my nails done by one of the girls in the salon, and I said to her, "I can't believe how much money I'm making. I was so poor before. This is great!"

She looked at me and said quietly, "Just watch your Ps and Qs. They can be fun, but I've known this family for a long time, and I like you. They're backstabbers. Shane's family is very jealous of everyone, and if they think you're doing better than they are, they'll find a way to sabotage you. They've done it to me, so just watch yourself."

Unfortunately, I had already said something to Shane's sister, mostly because I was so proud. She had always done well for herself, or at least that's what it looked like, so I thought she'd be happy for me and proud of me. Management was usually happy when the stylists were making money, at least, in the previous salons I'd worked in. It benefitted the salon. It usually meant the stylist would stay, and the owner would have steady income. I had no clue that there would be jealousy of any type. *Why would anyone be jealous of me?* A few months later, Shane's sister called me. "Hi Leah, I have exciting news! We've decided that we are doing away with the rentals and putting everyone on salary." Salons have different pay structures; some rent stations by the week or month, some pay commission, which typically is a fifty–fifty split with the salon providing all the supplies, and some pay a salary. Usually rent is the best situation to make the most money. So, this so-called "exciting news" was anything but.

"Since you're so good with color and chemical services, we'll start you at nine dollars per hour, which will be top dollar for you. The others will start a little bit less. Isn't it great?!" She was acting like this was such a big deal, but all I could think about was what the nail girl had said.

Panic-stricken, I said, "Oh, wow. I'm going to have to think about this. I don't think I can live on that kind of money. That's less than half of what I'm used to making." That would leave me with $360 per week, when I was used to making nearly double that. We moved into the apartment in September of 1991, and she told me this was going to be effective starting in November that same year. I was nearly in tears when I asked, "Why didn't you tell me earlier, before I got this apartment!? You know your brother isn't working, and now my rent is significantly higher." I had started out on commission until I was able to switch over to a rental situation. Now I had to find yet another salon to work in.

What a bitch! I should have known she'd screw me over. I should have never bragged about how much money I was making. The nail girl definitely called it.

I met a girl who came into our salon to tan, and she happened to have a salon in Hayward. I asked her if she had any spaces for rent, and lo and behold, she did. So, there I was in a new shop, starting all over from the beginning. Some of my clients followed me to the new salon, but it was almost like starting from scratch. I had to build a clientele.

The new place was more of a nail salon with a few hair-styling chairs. Shane's sister's shop had walk-ins, which made it nice because someone would always walk in needing some hair service. This salon didn't have that at all. The only rare walk-in was usually a street person carrying a brown bag with some Schnapps in it, but their money was just as good as anyone else's. The people who worked there were much more professional, so at least that was a good thing. The owner of the shop was going through an ugly divorce, and we connected instantly. I would ask her stuff about it and then compare it to what I was going through.

In early December, Shane was still calling the salon to make sure I was working and not fooling around. So, I was surprised and confused when he came home one day and said he and his brother-in-law had just been at the jewelry mart in San Francisco. He handed me a little box and said, "Hey babe, I want you to open this."

As I opened the box, my heart started to race. Inside was a little diamond ring. I wasn't sure what was happening and asked, "What is this? This isn't an engagement ring, is it?" I probably sounded very ungrateful, but, before he started acting jealous, we had looked at rings, and this didn't look like any of the ones I'd liked. We weren't even getting along. Not to mention, he had quit helping me with the bills. Yet now he was buying me jewelry? *What the hell?*

"Well?" he said.

"Um, I don't know what to say. Thank you. Do you think

we're really ready for marriage? Maybe this could be a promise ring or something until we're ready."

"I know things haven't been the best, but I want to be with you. If you want this to be a promise ring, then that's what it'll be. We'll get another ring when we get married." He said it with such genuine understanding and love that he must have been having a good day.

I had no intention of ever marrying him. I wanted him out of my life. But I somehow knew that I had to err on the side of caution. He was getting weirder and weirder, and I knew anything might set him off at any time.

Sure enough, the fighting continued, even though I had the stupid ring. How could we possibly marry each other? We didn't even like each other!

A couple of weeks later, I finally talked Shane into taking the deposit back, so he could move out. "I want that ring back!" He yelled.

"It was a gift, and it's mine," I replied. I planned on hocking it for the money that he owed me from not paying any bills. He took the nine hundred and fifty dollars, which was the deposit amount, stupidly put it in Brittany's diaper bag, which was tied onto his bicycle, and then left the house.

When he came home later that day, he said, "You're never going to believe this! Somewhere on my bike ride, I lost the diaper bag with the money you gave me to move out. Guess I'm staying. And you're just gonna have to deal with me, roommate."

"Why in the hell would you carry nine hundred and fifty dollars in a diaper bag on a bike ride? Are you serious?" My voice was quivering; I was about to cry, thinking, *You idiot!*

I didn't know what else to do. So, I went to the apartment manager to see about removing Shane from the lease "He's not paying any rent," I explained. "What can I do? He even put a hole in one of the doors."

"Since you are both on the lease, there's nothing we can do. If he doesn't pay, you still need to, or your credit gets affected." She was very kind in letting me know that I was screwed.

I finally talked to my mother about it and said, "Mom, I don't know what to do. He won't leave, and he fights with me all the time."

My mother was not the type of person for me to use as a shoulder to cry on. This was her chance to tell me I deserved it. She said, "You're a grown-up. Figure it out. You made your bed, now lie in it." I had seen these responses on television shows about abused women, and I felt like I was in a bad Lifetime movie. I had seen all those movies, like *The Burning Bed* and *Sleeping with the Enemy.* I wanted to know how the women in those film got out of their situation, because mine was looking like a truly fucked-up, abusive relationship.

I was hoping that if I was mean enough to Shane, he'd go away, so I told him whenever he left the house, "I hope you get hit by a bus and die. I *hate* you!" Even though I knew I shouldn't stoop to his level, I was so frustrated that I had gotten myself into this situation and couldn't get out, I just lashed out whenever and wherever I could. The straw that broke the camel's back was a fight around Christmas, not long after he gave me that ring. I said something that upset him, and he threw a bowl of cereal at me, which crashed into the wall. Then I hit him with some Christmas decorations. I was furious. He had recently bought a gun, which he had hidden upstairs in the closet. I was so pissed off that I went and got the gun and pulled it out on him. I took all but one of the bullets out of the gun. "Get the fuck out of my house! Don't make me kill you." I'd have done it in a heartbeat, if I'd thought I could get away with it. "I hate you. Just leave me alone!"

He grabbed me by the neck and ripped the gun out of my hands. "You fuckin' bitch! What the fuck is wrong with you?" After he took the gun, he ripped the cheesy promise ring off my finger and proceeded to call the cops. Thank God he didn't break my neck or my finger.

The cops came and yelled at me, "Where's the gun?"

"It's upstairs, put away." My voice was seriously trembling. I didn't know how much trouble I was about to be in.

"You're lucky that gun wasn't still in your hands or you'd be dead! We shoot at people that are threatening people with guns. But you are in serious trouble." He directed his conversation towards Shane, "Are you okay? Do you want to press charges?"

Everything was such a blur at that moment. I thought, *How did this happen to me? I thought I was at a low before, but this must be rock bottom. I could go to jail. He's been terrorizing me all this time, and now I'm in real trouble.* Nothing actually did happen to me, and I'm not sure exactly how this was reported, but I know there was something.

Shane made my life even more miserable, as if it could get worse. One night, he threw crayons at my head, like a child. I'd finally had enough and hit him as hard as I could over the head with the landline phone. I was hoping to knock him out, like in the movies, but that didn't go down very well. He picked me up and threw me against the wall. He was like Dr. Jekyll and Mr. Hyde. One minute he could be really nice, and his eyes would sparkle; I had recently watched the movie *Sybil* where Sally Fields plays a person with multiple personalities, and maybe I was being paranoid myself, but Shane had some of the same tendencies. I thought, *If he starts talking in the third person like Sybil does in that movie . . .*

I really started to think he was a bit more than just a possessive boyfriend. Something was really off, but I couldn't quite put my finger on it. His mood swings were much more extreme, and he was getting more paranoid and not just with me. He confided in me, "I called the DEA on my brother-in-law, and I think they are watching their house. I always see someone in a mail truck or a PG&E truck eating lunch by their house. I know they're undercover." I knew his brother-in-law sold pot, but I didn't think it was that big a deal. He was sharing more about himself and some of the abuse that he had endured as a child, and I almost felt sorry for him. I had heard stories of how this abusive stuff runs in families, and I didn't want that for my child; besides, this was way too much for me to handle.

I decided that maybe we should go to therapy to work on our situation. "Shane, how would you feel about going to couple's therapy? I really think it would be good for us." My goal was to show Shane that we were not good together, and this was so unhealthy.

"Yeah, babe, that would be a great idea. Then we can be together forever. I really love you."

Love? You have a funny way of showing it.

We found a male counselor which was a good thing, because I don't think Shane respected or liked women. The counselor thought it would be best to work with Shane individually at first. After their first couple of sessions, the counselor called me and asked, "What's your goal with Shane? He has some serious, deep-seated issues." I didn't understand it at the time, but the therapist must have thought I was in real danger.

"I can't be with him. He scares me, and I don't like him at all. I'm hoping he will understand and come to his own conclusion that we are not right for each other."

The counselor didn't seem surprised, "Well, we have to be very careful how we handle this. This might not be safe for you. I believe he has borderline personality disorder and suffers from deep depression. When he's down in what I call his deep hole, I think he might project hate onto you. I think we should get you out of this relationship, but I agree it needs to be his idea or he won't leave." The counselor actually scared me a bit, but I was glad someone was finally on my side.

It seemed like Shane enjoyed going to therapy. Whenever he got into a deep depression, he would accuse me, "Who is he? I know there's someone. I better never see him. I'll kill whoever gets between me and my family!" I have to say that going through all that, I learned that you should end one relationship before you start another. If I had cheated, I think that he might have killed me or the other person.

Whatever was happening in Shane's therapy, he was coming to the conclusion that our relationship probably wasn't good for his wellbeing, which was great for me, but I needed things to move more quickly. I began to pray harder than I ever had. I prayed so hard, telling God I would be willing to be alone for the rest of my life, if Shane went away. I really didn't want to be alone forever, but I would rather be alone than be stuck in that situation. I also made lots of phone calls to the therapist during the off hours. I think the therapist and the prayers saved me.

Finally, after five months of therapy and many prayers, Shane decided to move out. It was two weeks after Brittany's second birthday. That was one of the best days of my life. Freedom! Still, my dysfunctional self was a little sad. I wished things had been normal and worked out. When a woman is in an abusive relationship, the man always says, "No one will ever love you the way I do." And there was a part of me that believed it. I had a child with this person. *Is Shane right? Can someone love me when I already have someone else's child?* Not to mention I had prayed pretty hard to God, but now I wasn't sure that I really wanted to be alone forever.

Chapter 12

FREEDOM

I could finally breathe! I had my house to myself. *Thank you, God, for answering my prayers.* No more being terrorized by that crazy person. Brittany wouldn't have to live in such a dysfunctional household. Sure, in a perfect world, it would have been nice for Brittany to grow up with both parents, but that was never going to happen. I would never stay in a horrible situation for a child's sake. I knew from personal experience that wasn't good for the child. I'd rather be a happy single mother than be with someone who was unstable and always angry and with whom I fought constantly. How could that kind of environment be good for any child?

Now that I had this newfound freedom, I wanted to play. I wasn't ready for a "real" relationship, but I missed male attention. We all seemed to have a fallback person we called at times like these, and mine was my high school friend Teddy, the one with the crazy girlfriend with whom I got into a fight at the BART station. He was my rebound guy, and I was his rebound girl. Naturally, I called him, and we started to see each other. He had always been a lot of fun, a party guy who drank a lot. The drinking wasn't that bad, but he had started using drugs like crank and cocaine. He used to get mad at me for doing drugs. He had never done drugs before because he had a heart condition, but he started sometime in his early twenties. I wasn't sure if I liked him all that much on drugs, and I didn't want to be tempted. Although his personality had changed since high school, he was still pretty cute—but, the more we hung out, the more his issues surfaced. Boy, did he have a lot of issues. He had bad mood swings and had attempted suicide. He had also been through an ugly divorce. Since I was coming out of a totally fucked-up situation, I figured we could relate pretty well. Then the conversation took a turn while we were drinking. "Leah, I think I'm falling in love with you," Teddy confessed.

"Oh no, you're not. It's the booze talking. You know this isn't what we do." I knew we were too different, and, to me, he was a cute party guy with way too many issues. I had always been attracted to him physically, but he was unpredictable. One day he'd be up, and then next way down. When he was doing drugs, he would disappear, wouldn't answer my calls. And, of course, the more he ignored me, the more attention I gave him.

I had my own issues, and, as soon as the cat and mouse game started, I wanted him. He would pull away because I was showing too much interest in him. We were never on the same page at the same time. He was in love with me and I wasn't and vice versa. I also noticed that he had a look in his eye very much like Shane's. I couldn't quite put my finger on it until Brittany and I went to his birthday party at his parents' house, where Teddy had been living since his divorce.

His parents were both alcoholics. His mother was a mean

drunk and always picked fights or started crying over something. And his dad was in rare form the day of the party. He showed me and another girl a picture of him and said, "Hey, check this out."

"Uh, oh my!" I gasped and saw the same reaction on the other girl's face. We looked away as fast as we could, once we realized it was a naked picture of Teddy's father, and he was hung like a horse. I wished that I could erase that from my memory. This was not the kind of thing you should show your son's girlfriend, or anyone for that matter.

Once Teddy's mom figured out what had happened, all hell broke loose. She smacked her husband upside the head with a half-gallon of ice cream and yelled, "What the fuck are you doing? Are you trying to impress those young girls? They don't want you, you fucking old man!"

Teddy's face said it all. He charged after his mother and knocked her to the ground. I was screaming at Teddy, "Stop, Teddy, don't! Leave her alone!" I thought he was going to punch her lights out.

He was so angry and embarrassed. "What's wrong with you? You always ruin everything! I hate you!" But he didn't punch her. He went to his room, and I went after him.

"Are you okay?" I asked, and he looked at me with dark eyes, full of rage, and punched in the wall as if it were my face. I thought, *Holy shit, that looked like it was meant for me.* I knew right then that I had traded one fiery hell for another.

A few weeks passed when Teddy got arrested and wound up in Santa Rita County Jail, and that was pretty much the end of that relationship. Which was definitely a good thing.

I was left feeling a bit odd about my choices in men. I was

starting to put two and two together. *Why do I pick these violent guys? I wasn't raised that way.* Yet all my boyfriends had been violent in some way. Had I stayed with them long enough, I would have been a target. Teddy was pretty close, and it was just a matter of time. All my boyfriends had gone to jail at some point in the relationship. I needed to go back in therapy to get help breaking this pattern.

My new counselor was referred by the therapist who'd helped when I needed to get Shane out of my house. She told me I suffered from post-traumatic stress disorder brought about by my situation with Shane. She said this frequently happens to women who have been in abusive relationships. *What? I wasn't abused! I just lived with a psychopath. I wasn't beaten. I wasn't a victim! I can stand up for myself!* She hit a nerve for sure, and I was pretty offended. I had grown up knowing I could always stand up for myself, and here she was, making me feel like a "mark." Yet she also really got into my head and made me think I needed to try something new.

I had gotten into the pattern of having my eye on someone new whenever a relationship was ending. I started talking with Teddy Number Two, the brother of my friend from the Five and Dime. I called him Teddy Number Two to keep him straight from the first Teddy. He wasn't a criminal, and he dressed in suits. He was certainly different, and I thought that I should give him a try. The only thing was he didn't have a car, and he hid that fact for some reason. Well, old habits die hard, so I wasn't likely to pick a super great guy quite yet. Whenever we were going to go out, he'd always meet me in a parking lot in a strip mall or something. He'd be walking away from a nice car like a BMW, and I assumed it was his. One day, I was taking him back to the lot, and I asked, "Which car is yours? Is it that one?" I pointed to a BMW.

"No, that's not my car. Just drop me off over there," he replied nonchalantly.

"I thought you had a BMW? Where's your car? I'll drive you to it."

"Really, it's okay. I have to get something at that store."

After a few occurrences of that type of scenario, I began to think something was fishy. "Do you even have a car? I've never seen you get into one. And I'm always meeting you in a parking lot. What's up with that?"

"Well, I'm in the process of buying a car."

In the process? What twenty-something guy doesn't have a car? And if you don't have a car, why hide the fact? "So, you don't have a car?" I asked. "Why didn't you just say so? I don't care whether you have a car or not." I really didn't care. I thought it was a weird thing to hide. He paid for everything when we went out, so I couldn't care less if I did the driving.

I thought he was rich and successful. I wasn't sure what he did at the time for work, but he was always dressed in suits. I think he mentioned being in sales. Again, that stuff wasn't important to me. After all, he was the first guy I'd dated who wore suits and had credit cards. It was nice for a change.

I noticed that he would only see me on certain days and times. I knew he had a son from his previous marriage, but Teddy Number Two only saw his kid every other weekend, so that didn't account for all the other times he wasn't available. I figured he had another relationship going on the side, but it didn't matter much to me because I considered him an "in the meantime" kind of a guy.

He really blew it when we went out to dinner at Tito's Restaurant, and Brittany was a little cranky. She was usually really good in restaurants and other public places, but this evening I had forgotten her blanket or bottle, so she was acting out. Teddy Number Two told me, "You need to wear the pants and control your daughter while we're at a restaurant. My son would never act this way."

"Oh really?" I snapped. "I wear the pants, the skirt, and everything else! You're just a Disneyland dad, and when you're a full-time parent, like I am, then maybe, just maybe, you could say something." What a nerve. And just like that, another relationship went down the tubes.

Each guy I dated from that point on was a stepping stone. There was improvement in each guy, and there were a lot of stones. I managed to avoid drama, and I started seeing my Oakland girlfriends again. We went dancing and hung out in bars. My family babysat one night a week, perhaps hoping I'd find a suitable husband.

Not long after I started hanging out with my school friends, I ran into a guy named Paul at a party. He was so much fun and really social. Paul was the nice guy that everyone knew and loved. I remembered him from high school, and, even then, I thought he was cute. He made going out to bars or parties always fun. All my friends seemed happy for me, and I loved having their approval, because most of them hadn't thought much of my past relationships. I felt like I was in a decent place for once, like I was normal. I finally had someone I could go in public with who would not get jealous.

He was the perfect weekend boyfriend. He loved his work, which was landscaping, and he loved experiencing crazy adventures in other countries. He was the ultimate free spirit, and I totally admired that in him. He was always happy.

At first, my relationship with Paul was a bright spot in a strange time. A few months after he and I started dating, Brittany and I moved into my grandma's house to save money for a down payment on a house. I was twenty-four, I was an independent contractor as a hairstylist, renting a station in a salon, and was in a great relationship for a change. Unfortunately, there were a few rules for moving into Grandma's, including a curfew. On my one night out, I had to be home by one thirty. It sucked, but I understood why, and I was able to save money. Grandma charged me a certain amount of rent a month. She kept some of it for bills and saved the rest of it for when I was ready to move out.

But, as my twenty-fifth birthday approached, Paul and I got into a fight. It was St. Patrick's Day, and I wanted him to come over and hang out with me, since it wasn't my night to go out. But he had different plans, and, as he was telling me all the things he was going to do, I got a little bit jealous and said, "You're a horrible boyfriend."

He said, "If I'm so horrible, maybe we should just be friends."

"Fine," I agreed, hoping he would realize what an amazing person he was giving up. Well, that totally backfired.

I was particularly devastated by this breakup. I already felt like a loser living with my grandmother, being a single mother, and always being judged by others. When Paul and I were dating, Paul's grandpa told me, "You're so lucky to land a guy like Paul," as if I weren't worth it. I thought, *What does that mean? I'm a real catch.* I had saved up a lot of money, and I had goals which I was getting close to.

I never thought he was the cheating type, until I found out he'd cheated. I learned about it after we broke up. I was out at one of our local bars with my friends, and I saw Paul's father there. Naturally, I went up to him. "Hi, what brings you here?" I asked, in a genuine, friendly voice.

Looking around the room frantically, he said, "What are you doing here?"

"You know. The usual. I'm just getting out for a bit." I thought, *What's wrong with him and why is he acting so weird?* It didn't take me long to figure out why. In walked Paul with this girl named Diane, a girl that he and I had hung out with before, and they were acting a little bit too friendly with each other. I figured out that they were dating now and probably had been before we broke up. I would never have caught on if Paul's dad hadn't acted so strangely. I always knew that Diane and Paul were friends, because we had all double dated together. Apparently, Diane and her boyfriend had recently broken up. Not too long before Paul and I broke up, one of my friends said she had seen Diane and Paul together and thought I should know. I didn't think anything of it, because I thought she still had her boyfriend. But it all made sense as I put the pieces together.

As one relationship ended, I had a way of finding someone else. I ran into Scott's sister Jean, which got me thinking about how that whole thing had gone down. So, I asked her, "How's your brother? What's he been up to? Tell him I said hi." and Scott showed up in my life again. I had some unfinished business with him that I couldn't let go. He had become quite a loser, in all kinds of trouble with the law, but I had a game to win. I knew exactly what I was doing. I was going to ruin him like he had ruined me the night he had stolen my innocence. I didn't generally carry baggage from one relationship to another, but this was an unfinished relationship, and I needed to get even.

We dated for a very short time, and it was anything but exciting. Mostly, he'd ask if I wanted to go fishing, and we'd end up at Don Castro, a little lagoon in Hayward, at night so we didn't have to pay a parking fee or show a fishing license. I would much rather have been out with friends or at a party, but I tolerated the boredom to accomplish my end goal: to get him to fall madly in love with me, and then give him the ax.

When I began to sense that he was falling for me, I pulled away on purpose. I made plans with my friends and wasn't available as much. Predictably, the more I blew him off, the more he came around and wanted to be with me. Although his clinginess was a turn-off and I had no desire to be with him in the long run, I kept him on a string like he had done to me in the past. From time to time, I would give him a call to hang with him for an hour or so, and then withdraw again.

It was easy for me not to get attached to him this time, because I'd done some growing up, and the things that had attracted me to him in the past were no longer effective—such as the day Scott showed up at my house in a new-to-him Datsun 280Z. "You know, these are the easiest cars to steal," he bragged.

"Are you saying that you stole this car? What the hell?" I

couldn't believe this guy was almost thirty and still stealing things.

"What's the matter?" he said with complete sincerity, as if stealing was a good thing.

"When are you gonna grow up? You can't steal things forever. You're not even a good criminal. You always get caught." Which was so true. He *always* got caught—as his letters and phone calls from the State Correctional Facility or Alameda County Correctional Facility would later attest. I was embarrassed about associating with him.

One of the straws that broke the camel's back was when Scott called me from San Quentin and said he was nervous because some guy had been thrown over one of the balconies and died. "If this is making you nervous, why don't you get your shit together and quit doing things that land you in jail? Quit breaking the law." He didn't stay too long that time, and frankly I don't even know why he was arrested. As usual, he claimed he was innocent; I think it was a drug possession charge.

I felt free to say whatever I wanted to him, because I didn't care if he left or not. I wasn't into him like I had been before, and I felt good that he no longer had any power over me. I finally brought up the rape and my need to resolve it with him. During one of these phone calls, I said, "You know you raped me, right?"

"No, I didn't. You wanted it."

"Do girls who want it cry? You know I said no and was crying."

"Why are you bringing this up now? You know I love you."

That was all I needed to hear. I had absolutely no feelings for this guy anymore. I got to hurt him the way he had hurt me. I had cried over him in the past, and now it was his turn. I actually made him cry. "This isn't working for me. I don't think we should see each other anymore."

"Is there someone else?"

"No. This just isn't for me."

"I know there's someone else! You can't just get over me! I was your first, and I know how girls work."

Wow, I thought. *I really don't care that he was my first. I don't feel anything. Am I supposed to? I don't even have feelings for the person I had a child with. What would make him think that he was so special?* I had to ponder that for a moment, but then I knew that yes, I really was over him, no matter what he said.

And, just like that, it was done. I'd had my sweet revenge and left him with a broken heart. Of course, it wasn't quite over for him. He continued calling me collect from various correctional facilities, but I wouldn't accept the calls. One time he got smart and he had someone three-way call me, so the call wouldn't come as collect.

When I answered he said, "Hey, how come you won't take my calls?"

"What do you want from me? I'd take your calls if I wanted to talk to you," I replied coldly.

"You're never gonna believe where they sent me. I was in Pelican Bay for a couple of days." He seemed proud to have been in this notorious prison.

"How did you end up there? You must have done something really bad this time."

"No. The cops planted drugs in the car. I didn't have any."

"But you *do* sell drugs."

"But I didn't have any on me that day."

I just chuckled, thinking, *You idiot.* Then I said with a laugh, "I bet you were somebody's bitch."

"Why you gotta be like that?"

"Don't call me if you don't wanna hear stuff like that. You think that Pelican Bay would impress me? What's wrong with you? I suppose you're still innocent, too? Don't call me anymore. I don't have time for this bullshit."

Having that kind of closure was so fulfilling that I swore that I would never again go out with anyone who had been to jail or who didn't have a job. Things were going to be different, for real, this time.

I decided to channel all my energy into work, since I was good at setting goals and managing my finances. Our shop was working on visualization stuff. We read books like *The Seven Habits of Highly Effective People*, *Think and Grow Rich*, and *You Were Born Rich*. I have to say that I was pretty good at manifesting. The more I set my goals, the more things happened.

I joined a business networking organization called LeTip, where I met a realtor who saw a lot of potential in me and wanted to help. I told him I was saving up to buy a house, and we started to search. The realtor took me to look at many houses, even though I wasn't sure if I could handle an actual mortgage payment.

The realtor had a friend who wanted to offload his condominium. It was rented, but he was ready to sell it. It was in Castro Valley, but the school district was Hayward, which wasn't where I wanted Brittany to go to school, but that was still a few years off. Besides, I could use Grandma's address for a while like Mom had when my sister and I were children. I knew this was my starter home. I planned to live there for five years and then buy up.

There was some creative financing involved, so my parents and I sought legal advice to make sure it was on the up and up. All the paperwork was legitimate, so I bought my first house. In my family, you were considered an adult once you bought a home. My sister had bought her house at twenty-one. Now, not only could no one judge me, but I also knew firsthand that visualization and determination worked.

Right around that same time, in October, I was at a funeral for my high school friend Larry, when I spotted this really hot guy who was one of the pallbearers. He had long, curly hair tied back in a ponytail, and he looked like a rocker all dressed up in his suit. I thought I knew everyone in our little Oakland group, but I had never seen this guy before. I asked my friend Beth who he was.

She laughed and said, "That's Chris's brother, Travis." Chris was Beth's boyfriend, and I had heard of Travis before but had never seen or met him. He looked really good, the kind of good I fell for.

While we were at Larry's mom's house for the reception after the service, Chris came up to me with a shit-eating grin and said, "So, you think my brother is cute?"

Damn Beth, I thought. Chris was always stirring things up, and I didn't know how this would play out, plus this guy was married. Chris whispered something to Travis then Travis came up to me with a smile and in a flirty way introduced himself. He looked so deeply into my eyes that I wanted to turn away and leave.

I was really nervous and said, "Oh, hi. I'm Leah." My heart was pounding so hard. I could see Chris in the distance, laughing. I had to leave. I was too nervous, and I had to go back to work that day. I was really attracted to this guy, and I was so bummed because he was married, although I didn't see his wife at the funeral.

As soon as I got to work, I called Beth to find out the skinny. "So, what's up with this guy?"

"You are never gonna believe it! I found out he's actually separated from his wife, and they're getting divorced!"

"Seriously?" I said. "When did this happen? How come I've never seen him before? He's fricken' *hot!*" Beth was excited too, because she was dating Chris and we would be dating brothers.

There was a Halloween party coming up at the Montclair Golf Course, and I had a feeling Travis was going to be there. Chris was in on it, and I think he and his mom and dad wanted Travis's wife to go away, so he wanted Travis and me to hook up. Travis and Chris were going to a Stones' concert that night, but Chris assured me they would show up to the Halloween party later. I couldn't believe it, but I was getting sick. *Are you kidding me?* I thought. Sickness wasn't going to stop me.

I arrived at Beth's house feeling rotten, but I didn't want to miss out on meeting this guy. Somehow, I had this intuition about him. There was a connection that I couldn't explain but I could tell he was interested in me. And I wanted to find out just how interested. I told Beth, "I'll just drink a lot. After all, a lot of medicine contains alcohol."

She said, "I'll drink to that!" So we did a couple shots of

tequila then left for the party. The first part of the party was a bit blurry, probably from keeping the sickness away. Around eleven o'clock, I saw Chris and Travis walk in the door.

"They're here!" I said to Beth. "Act cool, like you don't see them. Make them come up to us." Sure enough, they came over to us while we were dancing.

"Hey, what's up? Remember me?" Travis said with a smile.

I was thinking, *Of course I remember you, duh.* But I had to play it cool, "Oh yeah, I met you the other day at Larry's service. That was so terrible." We made some small talk at the party, and then Chris told Travis that he was going back to his house with Beth. Travis asked, "You want to go back to my brother's house for a bit?"

"Sure." I was feeling it. I knew this guy was interested, and I thought he was beautiful. Beth and I drove over in my car. We hung out for a bit, and then I had to go home because I was still living at my grandma's.

Travis walked me to my car, "I had a really good time." As he reached in to kiss me, I was dying inside. I had been drinking earlier that night and had cottonmouth, and I really didn't want his first impression of me to be like that.

I pulled away and asked, "Aren't you married?" I think my reaction surprised him, because I don't think too many women would pull away from him. I know that I didn't want to, but had to because of my dry mouth.

Kind of puzzled answered, "I'm separated." Then he added, "Chris is having a barbecue tomorrow. Are you coming? Give me your number and I'll call you."

"Maybe. I'll have to see." Knowing how sick I was, I knew I probably wouldn't see him that soon, but I gave him my number anyway.

Sure enough, the next day I was so sick that I didn't have any voice at all, but that didn't dampen my enthusiasm when the phone rang and I picked it up and it was Travis. "Hey, what's up?" he said. "We're having this barbecue over here. I really want to see you again."

I'm so glad he called! I thought. I so badly wanted to go, but there was no way I was going anywhere. I needed to get better. So, in my raspy, barely audible voice, I said, "I wish I could, but I'm so sick, and I wouldn't want all of you to get sick. Maybe we could get together later, next week or something? I should be better by then." I told myself, *On the bright side, you don't want to appear too eager—let the guy come after you.*

"Okay, get better soon. I really want to see you," he said in the sweetest, most sincere voice. I couldn't wait for the weekend.

We saw each other every weekend and some weeknights until the day I moved into my condo, December 12. I had my whole working crew of friends to help me move, but no Travis. I couldn't get ahold of him that day. I was disappointed in him, but I had plenty on my mind about my move.

Rumor had it that his soon-to-be-ex-wife, LC, had found out that he was interested in someone else. After Travis and I had hung out for a while, I found out that LC was the one who'd initiated the divorce. I panicked at this, because I could tell that he wasn't completely over her. And they had two kids. I knew I couldn't compete with history and kids. This didn't set very well with me.

After I had moved in and everyone had left, my phone rang. "It's me. What's up?"

"Really? What's up with you? Where were you today? I thought you were gonna help me move."

"I was busy."

"Well, now I'm busy. I gotta go." And I hung up on him. He called back a few times, but I didn't pick up the phone.

He knew that he had screwed up, so he apologized profusely and even put together Brittany's Christmas present, a new bike. I thought things were going pretty well, but he was putting a little bit of distance between us. Christmas came and went. I got him a present, but he didn't get me anything.

Then New Year's came and went and no Travis. I hadn't heard from him at all. I finally called Chris to see what was going on, and it couldn't be worse. "I'm sorry, Leah," he said with such sincerity. "He went with LC to the snow up in Tahoe for a few days." My heart sank so low. "Are you still there?"

"Yeah." Holding back tears, I answered him quietly, "I have to go." And I hung the phone up and sobbed.

I knew I shouldn't have got involved with a married man, especially one who got dumped! I really beat myself up for this one. That was it. I would never see him again.

I guess his trip didn't go that well, because about a week later Travis called my house and left me several messages. I so badly wanted to call him back, but I didn't. He even called my work, but I wouldn't take his calls. Then, one night, he showed up my door with an overnight bag. "What are you doing here?"

"I just need to talk to you," he pleaded.

"You need to go. I can't do this."

"Please, let me in. I can explain."

"There's nothing to explain. Actions speak louder than words, and you clearly need to be with your wife!"

"We are separated, and I'm making a choice now."

I finally, reluctantly, let him in the door, "You really hurt me. I didn't want to get involved with you if you still had feelings for her, but you pushed your way into my life, and now this."

"I am so truly sorry. I know this doesn't fix things, but I really do care about you." I could tell that he was truly sorry, but that didn't make me feel better.

"What happened on your little vacation? Is she no longer that into you?"

"Well, I needed to try for my family. We didn't get along and we fought a lot. Our relationship is over, and I don't want to blow this with you. Please, will you give me another chance? I promise I won't hurt you again."

"I don't know . . ." But I had such a hard time resisting him. This was something I had never felt before, but my gut said I'd be making a mistake. I felt like I was second choice, but like an idiot, I forgave him.

Things were good right up until Valentine's Day. Then he did a total disappearing act. No phone calls, nothing. I called Chris once more, and he told me the brutal truth. "I'm so sorry, Leah. I can't believe he didn't have the balls to call you and tell you what's going on. He's back with LC, and they're trying to work it out. He's moved back in with her and the kids. I think you need to let this go."

"Oh, I thought so. Thank you for being honest with me," I said in a pathetic, trembling voice.

As I hung up the phone, it really hit me hard. I couldn't believe after all his pleading and carrying on that Travis had dropped me like a bad habit. I wouldn't see or hear from him for months. I had paged him to see if we could have some sort of dialogue about what happened, and the call back I got was from a woman, who said, "You better not call this pager again, you stupid bitch! If I ever see you, you're gonna be sorry." I thought, *How dumb is she? I'm no threat. He chose her.*

I spiraled into a depression over this guy. In my mind I knew this was ridiculous. *Leah, get a grip! You only dated this guy for three months. You couldn't have been in love. What's wrong with you?* Work was a great escape for me because it got my mind off him, but, on my days off, I had a hard time getting out of bed. I hadn't been this upset over Shane, and he was the father of my child. I didn't understand it. I did the best I could to get over him, to go out with other guys and hang out with my friends, but money was tight because of the condo.

This went on for about a year or so. I ran into Travis a few times in my favorite bar, which meant he'd gone there looking for me. I still liked him and all, but I wouldn't let him know it. He was sitting with my friends and made eye contact with me and said, "Hey, what's up?"

I was a smartass. "You and the missus get into a fight? Or did she let you out?"

"What's that supposed to mean?"

"Exactly what I said. I'm sure she'd have a problem with you being here with me."

"No. We didn't get in a fight. I'm hangin' with my bro. Can't I do that?"

"You can do whatever you want." I felt for sure there had been a fight and he was sniffing around.

Chris turned to me, "Hey, I have your car registration at my house for some reason. I found it outside. It must have fallen out that night you drove us all home a few weeks ago."

Immediately Travis says to me, "I'll bring it to you. By the way, you still getting your gas at the Chevron station? I saw you there and I saw you're still working at the same place."

"Are you stalkin' me?" I jokingly asked. I kind of liked it, but I did think it was a bit strange. Then I said, "When you get divorced, why don't you give me a call and, if I'm available, maybe we could give it another go."

"Oh, you think I'm gonna get divorced?" He got pretty defensive.

I said with complete confidence, "I don't think; I know. Like I said, give me a call when . . ."

About a month later, I guess he had something to prove. Everyone who knew me knew that I went to this particular bar on Friday nights. And, on this night, Chris greeted me at the door, which was very out of character for him. He never greeted anyone. He always waited for people to come to him. Plus, this wasn't where he hung out very often, so I knew something was up. I scanned the room and, lo and behold, I saw this little, dark-haired, pretty woman with blue eyes and immediately said to Chris, "Is that LC?" I had never seen her before, but my intuition was in high gear. I knew it was Travis's birthday, and he'd picked my bar to celebrate. I guess he needed a little excitement, but I wasn't fighting for anyone who didn't want me.

I stayed as far away from him as possible. A lot of my

friends were there, since I was a fixture on Friday nights, so I completely ignored Travis and LC. Then I had to go to the bathroom. My friend wouldn't go with me, and I knew LC was watching my every move. Beth had warned me about LC, saying she was tough and I needed to be careful. I looked at LC and thought, *I could drop-kick this bitch in a hot minute; my friends have no faith in me.* I went into the bathroom, and she was right behind me. She started talking to another girl in there and then looked me up and down as if to size me up. I looked her right back in the eye and smiled smugly, as if to say, *Lady, you don't scare me.*

I went out and told my friends about our encounter, and I didn't realize she was right next to me. She ran her shoulder into Beth's sister and shoved her hard. I laughed and said loudly enough for LC to hear, "I'm sorry, I think that shove was meant for me."

I went over to the other side of the room, and I noticed that Travis was talking to his friend and pointing in my direction. Finally, I went up to him and asked, "What the hell are you doing?"

"What do you mean? I'm not doing anything."

"What's the matter? You having a little midlife crisis and need an ego boost? You think there's gonna to be some sorta catfight? Why don't you keep yo' bitch on a leash, 'cause if she follows me into the bathroom again, I'll kick her ass!"

"What?" He was clearly playing dumb, and she saw us talking, which totally flipped her out. It looked like she was yelling at him.

"Happy birthday, Travis! Bye-bye!" I blew him a kiss as they left abruptly. I was sad it had turned out like this and mad because I felt used again. They must have had makeup sex, because about a month later I found out she was pregnant with her third child. I was devastated once again, because even when they did get a divorce, he'd have too much baggage for me. It was truly the end of Travis and me.

After Travis, I had a new pattern, but this new pattern wasn't very good, either. It seemed to be the guys that I went out with weren't quite over their exes. I was the rebound girl. *If you want to get back with your ex, just date Leah, and she'll come back to you in no time.* I really had to change my ways because I was still the common denominator, just in a different equation.

I was sick and tired of being sick and tired. I had to do something. And then it came to me. At the salon, we were getting even deeper into personal development, and I began to realize that I had a strong pattern of manifesting. I thought, *If I could manifest a house, maybe I can focus on finding a good guy.* I still needed to figure out specifically what that man would look like, but I knew he was going to meet higher standards. I was going to make sure this new guy truly deserved me, and he would need to prove that before I got physical with him. This was my New Year's resolution.

Chapter 13

IS THERE A REASON FOR ALL THIS?

My first step in pursuit of my New Year's resolution was to get away from my usual haunts, especially my regular bars, as well as far away from the people who had shattered my self-esteem.

In a club in Santa Clara one night, I met a guy who seemed pretty interesting, more along the lines of the kind of man I was hoping to connect with. I gave him the third degree and even asked him if he had a criminal record. He was going to be a physician's assistant, bought me drinks, and seemed like an upstanding young man. Unfortunately, old habits die hard. You don't completely change overnight. After a few dates, it came up in conversation that he in fact had been arrested for stealing and maybe wasn't quite in the right classes to become a PA. While we were on a date at his house, some girl showed up and turned out to be his recent ex-girlfriend, whom he wasn't quite over. I knew right then and there this new guy was over for me. I was not going to go through any of that bullshit. I was sticking to my guns on my vow to myself that I wasn't going to be with anyone who wasn't worthy.

However, that mishap was just irritating, not devastating, and it was not going to stop me from going out and finding someone I'd be compatible with. About four months later, my ex Paul—the first decent guy I'd gone out with and now a friend—called to invite me to a plant sale that he was planning to have at his friend Hunter's place, right near my house.

"I haven't seen any signs for it," I said. "Hunter should put some up at the back gate of my complex."

"He's with me now. Here, talk to him. You've met him before, right?"

"I don't think so, but put him on the phone."

I heard a voice say, "Hi, I'm Hunter, and Paul just handed me the phone."

"Hi, I'm Leah. So, you guys should hang up signs at the back gate of Mesa Verde. You know the condos that are right next to the freeway and Foothill? I bet you'd get a lot of people from here going to your sale."

"Thanks. Are you coming to the sale?"

"No, I'm actually going to a wedding that weekend outta town. Otherwise, I would love to. Paul always has good stuff." That was pretty much the extent of it. I didn't give any of this much thought.

A few weeks after the wedding, a group of us were going to meet up at the local dive bar in Castro Valley. Paul was coming and mentioned he was bringing Hunter. I asked one of my friends, "Hey, do you know Hunter? I talked to him on the phone about a plant sale. Paul acted surprised that I didn't know him. He seemed nice on the phone, but what's up with this guy?"

She just about came unglued, like she'd had some major epiphany. "Oh my God! Why didn't I think of this? Yeah, I know him. Remember when I told you about a party a few weeks ago? It was at his sister's house. He's totally cool. Super chill and nice. And he has long hair." She was so playing matchmaker, and my curiosity was really piqued. She had always been a goody-goody—the one who had a college degree and picked non-delinquent boyfriends. She had a good sense of what I liked as far as looks. Plus, she had known me since high school and knew that I was trying to better myself, meaning finding a nice, decent guy.

"Well, he's coming to the bar tonight," I told her, but did not add, *We'll see.*

Everyone showed up at the bar, Doucet Saloon, as planned. Paul immediately walked up to our group and introduced me to Hunter. It was clear that everyone except me knew him, but I was trying to think if I had seen him before. He looked so much like this other guy that I had sort of known, but I guess that didn't really matter. "Hi, nice to meet you." Hunter said. He had a great smile with perfect teeth, and he did have long hair, which I was definitely attracted to. We all hung out playing pool and shuffleboard, but nothing seemed out of the ordinary. It was getting late, and we all left the bar. Hunter and Paul walked to Paul's car, and I was heading toward mine when Paul pulled up next to me. Hunter had his head hanging out of Paul's car window, as if to make a point, and said again, "It was really nice to meet you."

I smiled back and yelled, "It was nice to meet you, too!"

although I thought, *Hmm, how come he didn't ask for my number? He seems interested now, but am I getting mixed signals? What just happened?*

About a couple of weeks had gone by, Teddy Number Two had a birthday and wanted to go to my neighborhood bar for a drink. We were still friends, so I agreed. Thank God, because my friends were going to meet up there as well. Then guess who walked in the door? Of course, Hunter. I had never seen him there since that night he had shown up with Paul, so I thought he might have come to see if I was there. *Maybe he really is interested in me*, I allowed myself to think.

Shortly after he arrived, he came right up to me and Teddy Number Two, "Hey, how's it going?" He asked, with his beautiful smile and perfect teeth.

"Hi, I didn't know you were coming!" I was hoping I wasn't showing too much excitement or looking like I was desperate or anything. "This is my friend Teddy. It was his birthday, so I thought I'd buy him a birthday drink. How was your plant sale?"

"It was good; we sold a lot of plants. So, what's been going on with you? I know we didn't get a chance to really talk last time."

Although Hunter seemed interested and ready to really engage with me, poor Teddy wanted all the attention and tried to butt in. "Hey, Leah, I got this new job. Did I tell you about it?"

But I was done with Teddy, and I turned over to talk to Hunter, "I know. So, where exactly do you live? I remember you saying it was pretty close to my house." I had other ideas. I wanted to pursue this new guy. I had heard of him but never had seen him around my group. He seemed smart and confident, which was a good sign—not to mention that he lived less than a mile from me.

We talked about everything. I even told him how I was devastated over Travis, which probably wasn't the best idea, but I was drinking pretty heavily. I figured I let it all out and if it was meant to be, then *que será será*. I was pretty bold; I gave him a big, flirty grin and said, "Here's my number. You should call me sometime." He gave me his number, too, but I wasn't going to chase him. I made it very clear that I was interested, and he could chase me if he wanted.

Sunday came, and guess who called? "Hi. I really enjoyed meeting you," Hunter said. "Would you be interested in going out sometime?" I was so excited. He didn't act desperate and seemed normal.

"Sure. That sounds like a great idea."

We planned to go out to dinner the following Friday, which happened to be the day before Brittany's sixth birthday party. I had a lot of energy back then. I made a bunch of cupcakes the day of my date with Hunter. Brittany was spending the night at my mom's house, because I had to work in the morning before the big barbeque birthday at Chabot Park.

Hunter and I went to Don Jose's, the Mexican restaurant in town, on our first date. And we happened to run into his oldest sister, who, thank God, didn't make the situation awkward. She just said hi, introduced herself briefly to me, and then excused herself.

Once Hunter and I were settled alone at an outdoor table, I asked him a lot of questions. "So where do you work? How many brothers or sisters do you have?" I had already spilled my guts at the bar. I'd probably shared too much, but we knew a lot of the same people, and I didn't want to look like I was hiding anything.

He answered all my questions. "Well, I have three sisters and a brother, and you probably know some of them." I remembered meeting his brother in high school, but I was very stoned at the time. I knew of his sisters, but didn't know them personally. "I am a carpenter, and I moved into my duplex about a year ago. It's a work in progress, but I like it. So, you have a daughter? My sister that you just met has twins."

We were talking about family, and I knew you could tell a lot about a person by how they got along with their family. He proceeded to tell me a little of his family dynamic. "Well, two of my sisters aren't my blood siblings. My mother passed away when I was ten, and my dad got remarried. We really don't use the word *step* except I refer to my stepmom by her name."

"I'm sorry about your mom. Was she sick?"

"Sort of, you could say. She suffered from mental illness, manic depressive disorder, and she took her own life."

"Oh, my. I'm really sorry, I didn't mean to pry."

"It's okay, I was in lots of therapy as a kid, and I can talk about it. My dad had us kids in counseling, plus, I'm pretty close with my dad. And I was a bit of a terror for my stepmother, having anger issues and all, but we kids were always close, and we had a lot fun and happy memories. So, it's all good."

We finished dinner, and neither of us wanted to end the night, but I didn't want to come off as too aggressive. He said, "Would you like to come over to my house for a drink?"

"Sure." I was glad he asked. I felt things were moving

along in a good direction. We went back to his place for a nightcap, and I got to meet his big-ass Rottweiler, Rocco. If a dog could be a dick, he was one. I think that Rocco got extreme pleasure out of scaring the shit out of people. It brought up the old memories from the hill with the dogs. I wasn't deathly afraid or anything, it just made me think of all the other encounters I've had with dogs. After a while of just talking, Hunter took me home, walked me to my door, and said, "Goodbye."

"Goodbye." *Really? That's it? Goodbye? What did that mean? I thought he was interested, not even a kiss or peck?* I had no idea how to react. *I need another date with him.*

Since Brittany's party was the next day, I didn't know if it would be too weird or awkward for Hunter to come. I had a lot of kids from Brittany's school, family, and friends coming, so he'd know some people. I had told Paul about it and was really hoping Paul would bring Hunter to this party.

Even Shane, Brittany's biological dad, was invited. I never knew when he was going to come around. I wouldn't hear from him for months on end, and then one day he'd show up at my work wanting to see Brittany. In this particular case, he called me up with an accusation: "You know, you never let me see my daughter. How come you didn't invite me to my own daughter's birthday?" One of his sisters must have told him about it, since I had sent them an invitation.

"I don't know how to reach you, but if you want to come, then come. I'm not stopping you."

"Didn't it already happen?"

"No. Why would I have had it already? Her birthday falls on a Saturday this year."

"Isn't it the fifth?"

"You have a son with a birthdate the day before your daughter's, and you still can't remember it? Wow!" *How do you forget your child's birthday? This ought to be interesting if Hunter shows up. He'll get to meet everyone from my parents to my ex. Yay!*

———

The day of the party, Hunter arrived with a rose and handed it to my daughter, saying, "This is for you, Brittany. Happy birthday and nice to meet you."

It melted my heart. How sweet was that? I couldn't contain my excitement. "You came!" I said to him. "I'm so happy to see you."

Everyone else I had invited came, too, including Shane. I took Hunter around to everyone and introduced him. Everyone was very welcoming to him; even Shane didn't act like a jerk. Hunter is one of the mellowest guys in the universe. He was chill the whole time and didn't ever seem awkward in the slightest. If he could handle that, well, this would be the beginning of a beautiful relationship.

Hunter and I began seeing each other every day. And every day he came over, he brought freshly picked roses for Brittany and me. We did lots of things that included Brittany, like going to the movies or the zoo and playing peewee golf.

Between his kindness to my daughter and the fact that he was so easy to talk to—and actually listened to and remembered the things I said—I knew he was the one I would marry. I was so sure of it, I wrote it down a week after our first date.

It's very true when people say that you know right away—although that idea is not to be confused with merely *hoping* someone will be the one, as I'd done in the past.

He knew right away as well, he told me later. It wasn't long before we had "the talk." He was the one who initiated it: "So, where do you think this is going? Do you have plans to go out with other guys? Cause I'm not really into that. I like to focus on one person and go from there."

"I fully agree with you. I'm not interested in dating anyone else. I'm not into that either."

And just like that, we were officially exclusive. I treated this relationship very differently from those I'd had in the past, primarily in terms of my physical boundaries. I told Hunter, "Even though we're exclusive now, I want to take things slow and really get to know you before I give up the goods. I'm doing things differently than I have in the past, and hope you're okay with that." I would not sleep with him right away. I kept that promise that no one is going to have me, unless they are worthy.

"No problem. Let's take it slow." I believe he liked that I didn't just rush into anything physical fast. I think he respected me more for it. Although, the poor guy, I put him through the ringer. I was surprised that he put up with my drama.

Even though I believed I didn't bring baggage into a new relationship, I soon discovered that I had a lot of baggage I wasn't even aware of. All of the experiences I'd had were all coming out. First, I realized that I drank much more than he did. He wasn't a huge partier like I was. It didn't seem to bother him at first, though. We finally became intimate, and

I'm sure I was having some sort of cocktail, because I didn't even know how to have an intimate relationship without drinking. I felt so vulnerable and uncomfortable that the only way I could be with anyone was when I was drinking. I hadn't ever experienced a healthy relationship up to that point. I had no clue what a healthy relationship was. I wasn't used to boyfriends treating me so nicely. I knew my thinking on the subject was skewed, so I kept going with the relationship. Deep down, I knew Hunter was right for me, that he was going to enhance my life. He was great with my daughter, as well. But because I was going against my usual pattern, I think I was trying to sabotage my relationship with him.

When we had been going out for several months, I needed to get some drama going. Things were way too easy. We ate dinner at my house quite a bit, and, one night, I started thinking that I was doing all the cooking and cleanup, and I wasn't going to take care of anyone and get stuck like I did with Shane. "Can't you do the dishes for once?" I demanded. "We always mess up my house. I'm not a maid, you know." As soon as the words were out of my mouth, I thought, *I can't believe I said that to him. I was such a bitch.*

"Why are you yelling?" he said calmly. "I'll help you right now if you'd like. In fact, I help you quite a bit. I pick up Brittany for you all the time. So, I'm not sure where you're coming from. Maybe I should just go." And then he left. This happened more frequently as we appeared to be getting closer, but, in reality, I was pushing him away.

Understandably, Hunter got so frustrated that he eventually broke up with me. I had been sure I had him wrapped around my pinky—until he said, "I love you very much, but you can't treat me like this. I will be sad, but I *will* get over you!"

Those words have lasted forever. I will never forget them as long as I live. As twisted as I was, that was the best thing that he could ever have said. It was actually a turn-on, because I gained so much respect for him. Deep down, I was beginning to realize I didn't actually want a guy I could walk all over. I knew I had truly hurt him, and I was being a completely selfish bitch. I knew I had blown the best thing that ever happened to me, and I had to do something different from what I had been doing. This was the best relationship I had ever had, and I had to fix it! But I had been so broken for so long, I just didn't know what to do. I went to his house and pleaded, "Can we talk? I really miss you." And I started to cry.

"Talk about what? I think you need some help. You've been mean, and I don't deserve that. I've treated you well."

"I know you have. I don't know what's wrong with me. I'm not used to all of this."

"I think maybe you drink a bit too much. You want to go out with your friends and party all the time, and I'm not really down with all that. If that's what you want to do, I'm not getting in the way. It's cool."

"I'm not really into that. Maybe sometimes, but I want to be with you much more than I want to be with them. I know I've been terrible. I'm so sorry. I really am. Please, will you give me another chance?"

After a pause that seemed like an hour of cold silence, he said very sincerely, "Okay, I'm going to give you one more chance, because I know there is much more to you. I see what a great job you've been doing as a single mom and how well you take care of business, and you're still fun." He came over and hugged me and he kissed my forehead. "I really care about you and love you, but I won't be treated badly."

"I love you too. I won't screw this up again. I promise," I said.

After that, we grew closer and closer, and, after we had been dating for eight months or so, the discussion of marriage came up. We knew we both wanted to get married, and he wanted more children, which was fine with me. I was still young, and I knew that was in my future. After a year of going out, he asked me to move into his place. We both owned our places, so I rented my condo and moved into his duplex to consolidate our bills. I was definitely better with money than he was, so I told him I'd pay all the bills as long as he paid the mortgage. He had never lived with a woman before and had never intended to unless he was engaged. Needless to say, we started ring shopping.

A month after living together and finding a ring, Hunter proposed to me. I had known for a long time that I wanted to be with this man forever. He would make me a better person, and, hopefully, I'd make him a better person. Of course, I said yes. My parents, family, and friends were so excited for me. I think my family was relieved that I had finally found someone to settle down with who would keep me out of trouble.

Wedding plans began. We planned on getting married on September 20, 1998. That gave us about a year and a half to plan. We picked the 20th because both of our birthdays were on the 20th, his on August 20 and mine on March 20. Isn't that romantic?

Meanwhile, it had been almost a year since I'd heard

from Brittany's biological father. Then, Shane showed up at my work one day, demanding to see his daughter and asking how I dared to keep her away from him. That was absolutely not true. I had given him plenty of chances to see her. I had put some stipulations on his visitations, but only because she was old enough to get her feelings hurt when he got her hopes up by saying that he was coming to see her and then didn't. I had seen too many kids get screwed up in the head over that, and I was not going to let it happen to my own child.

When Shane showed up at the salon, he was wearing a suit and talking about this church he was attending. That was a big red flag for me. He said it was just a nondenominational Christian church, which was what my church was growing up. Because of my childhood on Holy Hill, I knew how those churches operated. They usually stuck up for men or at least the churchgoer and would do whatever it took to get new members. I saw how this situation with Shane would all go down: the church would give him money for an attorney, and he and the lawyer would try to take Brittany from me. However, what no one might have known was that Shane couldn't take care of himself, let alone our daughter. Sometimes he even lived in his car! How was a child supposed to live that way?

I was petrified and immediately told Hunter about the whole incident and said I needed to talk to a lawyer. I got a referral from one of my clients and set up an appointment. We were told that a stepparent adoption was our best option. First, we had to have been married for a year before anything could take place. Second, they would ask Brittany if she was okay with the situation. Third, we had to contact the biological father to let him know what was happening. The third part was the hardest. I would have to give notification in a newspaper that this was all going to happen, and, because Shane moved around so much, I didn't know which paper to run the ad in.

Brittany was excited for Hunter to be her daddy, so that was not a problem whatsoever. And, although Hunter and I were already planning our wedding, we needed to be married to get this ball rolling. We moved up the date and kept the wedding plans going. The first day for a wedding in the court was on Tuesday, October 21, 1997. No one wants to get married on a Tuesday. But that's what we did!

The only ones who knew were my parents, Hunter's parents, and my grandma. Not even Brittany knew. We didn't want her spilling the beans. And I didn't want Shane to find out. I wasn't sure what he would do. I was hoping he'd just stay away for another year or so. In order to do a stepparent adoption, I had to prove that Shane had abandoned Brittany. The law states that if there was no child support and no visits in one year during any part of the child's life, it would be grounds for child abandonment. Shane never paid child support, and he went a long time without seeing her; I was pretty sure it had been a full year or so. It was hard to keep track because he moved around so much.

Keeping our secret was hard for me, because I was so excited to be married. An opportunity came up in March of 1998 for Hunter and me to buy a house from my grandmother. My grandma had inherited the house across the street from hers. It was in Castro Valley School District, and, frankly, I hated living in the duplex. It was small, and I really didn't like the neighborhood for children. I had even told Hunter when I moved in with him that I would only live there for two years. Then we would get a place in Castro Valley near Brittany's school, so I wouldn't have to lie about where we lived. My kid was *not* going to Hayward schools. That district was at least as bad as, or even worse than Oakland.

The law of attraction works so well! It hadn't been two years when this came about. Let's see, should we spend money on a wedding day or should we spend money on a lifetime new home? It was a no-brainer. On my birthday, we made the announcement that we had gotten married. Boy, did we have some people upset! We really didn't mean to, but we were doing what was best for Brittany.

Despite the frustration we caused, I was so glad that we'd announced we were married, because, about four weeks later, I discovered I was pregnant. Believe me, it didn't take much to get me pregnant. When Hunter confessed that he feared he might be sterile, I reassured him that I was probably fertile enough for both of us.

Within two and a half years, especially the last eight months of 1998, my whole world changed. We announced our marriage in March; in June, we bought a house and moved in; and we welcomed a beautiful, bouncing baby boy, Jason, just four days before Christmas. But change is good. Growth is good. At twenty-nine, I'd been through all my most challenging experiences up to that point, or so I thought: a crazy, fearful childhood, with guns, violence, a crazy cult, witnessing my friends suffering from physical and sexual abuse, a tragic fire, murder, overdosing, date rape, diseases, having a child alone, tons of rejection throughout my childhood carrying over to young adulthood, then ultimately finding true love. I had overcome my fears at a pretty young age; not much scared me anymore. I could face anything, and tackle any challenge.

Now, at age thirty, I was given a new beginning in the form of a happy family life. The struggle was over. Not only had I managed to stay alive and become a real grown-up, but I was living the American dream. My family could finally rest, knowing that I had a solid family of my own. I had finally made them proud, and they no longer had to worry about me. I had a husband who supported me and could take care of me. I knew I was strong and could take care of myself, that I really didn't *need* anyone. I *wanted* someone to share my life, though—a companion, a life partner. Needing and wanting that were very different.

I had gone through most of my life trying to prove myself and prove that I was a worthy person. Why was it so ingrained in me that I wasn't worthy? After all, I had bought my own home at twenty-five as a single parent. I had my own thriving business as a hair stylist and finally was capable of being in a healthy relationship. I had lots of successes in my life. I had even learned that the law of attraction works to get things. But that was just it: *things.* Something was still missing, but I couldn't pinpoint it. The only thing that I believed was a true accomplishment and that stuck with me through the years was overcoming my fears. One of the greatest gifts I was given was the chance to learn to face my fears and not hide from them.

Now I can face any confrontation. I don't particularly like confrontation, but it is a part of life. Had I not had such crazy experiences growing up, I'd probably still be that fearful little girl inside. Not to mention that I probably would not have been adequately prepared to have a husband and children of my own.

I am thankful and very lucky to end up in such a wonderful marriage with someone so "normal" (whatever that really means)—not a jailbird or an abuser of any kind. It's here where the real in-depth discoveries are being made. But as we know in the "real" world of marriage, nothing is perfect. This is the part of the journey that lets you contemplate, *Why are we all here? There must be a purpose for all this.* There has to be! Otherwise, why do issues that I've supposedly already overcome keep coming up?

I know there is a reason for it all. I believe these life challenges help our souls evolve to a higher level, even if my little human mind can't quite piece everything together at the moment. I have realized who my soul mates have been (and are) and how they are placed strategically to help me—the ones who are put into your life to help you discover what it is that you came on this planet to do. There's nothing like the closest people in your life to challenge you, especially your children. After all, you really are only as happy as your unhappiest child.

I believe our purpose on this earth is to evolve and grow. We all have life lessons to learn and life goals to fulfill. I have come a long way in the school of hard knocks, and I'm lucky that I didn't get seriously hurt or killed in the process. I'm sure this isn't the end of my learning, but I can appreciate all the positive changes I've already made. I know now that I have the tools to overcome any new obstacles that may present themselves in the next chapter of this life. "Bring it on!" I say.

ACKNOWLEDGMENTS

I have to thank so many wonderful people who have helped me in this process. First of all, my clients, for suggesting that my stories were interesting and that I should write. None of this would have happened if it weren't for my friend Barbara Tavres, who read my unedited manuscript, liked it, and introduced me to Brooke Warner from She Writes Press; Brooke, for giving me the steps and honest guidance to make the possibility of writing a book into a reality; Annie Tucker, for "Show me, don't tell me!" coaching and making my writing come alive; my copy/editor Robin for all that she has done; Crystal Lee Patriarche and Savannah Harrelson, my publicists for getting my book into the world; Lauren Wise, for managing all of this; my new She Writes Press sisters who are always willing to offer help from their experiences; believe it or not, the church for giving me faith and some interesting stories; even my elementary school, for toughening me up; my husband, Matthew, for never questioning me and always letting me be me and loving me; my children, Samantha and Kyle, for being awesome kids; Grandma, for her unconditional love and her wisdom; my sister Rohnda for not freaking out when I aired our dirty laundry; my friends, Melissa, Robin, Lisa, and Julie, for being in my life and sharing some crazy experiences; and all the other people who have helped in the manifesting of me.

Leah E. Reinhart is a hairstylist, angel card reader, and now author of her first book, *Manifesting Me: A Story of Rebellion and Redemption.* Conversation and great storytelling have always been a huge part of her life, so it seemed only natural for her to put her stories on paper. She has grown to love writing and will continue to write more books. She currently lives in the San Francisco East Bay, Castro Valley, California, with her husband, her nineteen-year-old son, and her furry babies.

SELECTED TITLES FROM SHE WRITES PRESS

Uncovered: How I Left Hassidic Life and Finally Came Home by Leah Lax. $16.95, 978-1-63152-995-5. Drawn in their offers of refuge from her troubled family and promises of eternal love, Leah Lax becomes a Hassidic Jew—but ultimately, as a forty-something woman, comes to reject everything she has lived for three decades in order to be who she truly is.

The S Word by Paolina Milana. $16.95, 978-1-63152-927-6. An insider's account of growing up with a schizophrenic mother, and the disastrous toll the illness—and her Sicilian Catholic family's code of secrecy—takes upon her young life.

The Coconut Latitudes: Secrets, Storms, and Survival in the Caribbean by Rita Gardner. $16.95, 978-1-63152-901-6. A haunting, lyrical memoir about a dysfunctional family's experiences in a reality far from the envisioned Eden—and the terrible cost of keeping secrets.

Fourteen: A Daughter's Memoir of Adventure, Sailing, and Survival by Leslie Johansen Nack. $16.95, 978-1-63152-941-2. A coming-of-age adventure story about a young girl who comes into her own power, fights back against abuse, becomes an accomplished sailor, and falls in love with the ocean and the natural world.

Learning to Eat Along the Way by Margaret Bendet. $16.95, 978-1-63152-997-9. After interviewing an Indian holy man, newspaper reporter Margaret Bendet follows him in pursuit of enlightenment and ends up facing demons that were inside her all along.

Not Exactly Love: A Memoir by Betty Hafner. $16.95, 978-1-63152-149-2. At twenty-five Betty Hafner, thought she'd found the man to make her dream of a family and cozy home come true—but after they married, his rages turned the dream into a nightmare, and Betty had to decide: stay with the man she loved, or find a way to leave?